Basket-Maker Caves of Northeastern Arizona

Also from Westphalia Press

westphaliapress.org

The Idea of the Digital University

Dialogue in the Roman-Greco World

The History of Photography

International or Local Ownership?: Security Sector Development in Post-Independent Kosovo

Lankes, His Woodcut Bookplates

Opportunity and Horatio Alger

The Role of Theory in Policy Analysis

Natural Gas as an Instrument of Russian State Power

Non Profit Organizations and Disaster

The Idea of Neoliberalism: The Emperor Has Threadbare Contemporary Clothes

Social Satire and the Modern Novel

Ukraine vs. Russia: Revolution, Democracy and War: Selected Articles and Blogs, 2010-2016

James Martineau and Rebuilding Theology

A Strategy for Implementing the Reconciliation Process

Issues in Maritime Cyber Security

Growing Inequality: Bridging Complex Systems, Population Health and Health Disparities

Designing, Adapting, Strategizing in Online Education

Gunboat and Gun-runner

Pacific Hurtgen: The American Army in Northern Luzon, 1945

New Frontiers in Criminology

Understanding Art

Homeopathy

Fishing the Florida Keys

Iran: Who Is Really In Charge?

Contracting, Logistics, Reverse Logistics: The Project, Program and Portfolio Approach

The Thomas Starr King Dispute

Springfield: The Novel

Alchemy: Ancient and Modern

Lariats and Lassos

Mr. Garfield of Ohio

The French Foreign Legion

War in Syria

Naturism Comes to the United States

Feeding the Global South

The History of Men's Raiment

Basket-Maker Caves of Northeastern Arizona

Report on the Explorations, 1916-17

by Samuel James Guernsey and Alfred Vincent Kidder

WESTPHALIA PRESS
An imprint of Policy Studies Organization

Westphalia Press
An imprint of Policy Studies Organization
1527 New Hampshire Ave., NW
Washington, D.C. 20036
info@ipsonet.org

ISBN-13: 978-1-63391-615-9
ISBN-10: 1-63391-615-4

Cover design by Jeffrey Barnes:
jbarnesbook.design

Daniel Gutierrez-Sandoval, Executive Director
PSO and Westphalia Press

Updated material and comments on this edition
can be found at the Westphalia Press website:
www.westphaliapress.org

PAPERS

OF THE

PEABODY MUSEUM OF AMERICAN ARCHAEOLOGY AND ETHNOLOGY, HARVARD UNIVERSITY

Vol. VIII. — No. 2

BASKET-MAKER CAVES OF NORTHEASTERN ARIZONA

Report on the Explorations, 1916–17

BY

SAMUEL JAMES GUERNSEY

AND

ALFRED VINCENT KIDDER

FORTY-FOUR PLATES AND SIXTEEN ILLUSTRATIONS IN THE TEXT

CAMBRIDGE, MASSACHUSETTS, U. S. A.
PUBLISHED BY THE MUSEUM
1921

INTRODUCTION

In the summer of 1914 the Peabody Museum of Harvard University sent an expedition to northeastern Arizona under the joint leadership of the present authors for the purpose of studying the relations between the cliff-houses of that district and those of the north side of the San Juan River. In the course of this trip, evidence was found of the presence of the Basket-maker culture. This culture had hitherto only been reported from a single rather restricted area in southeastern Utah.[1] Furthermore, no Basket-maker remains had ever been taken out by trained investigators; so that the claims, put forward by the commercial collectors who discovered and named the culture, that it was a distinct one, antedating that of the Cliff-dwellers, had been received by archaeologists with more or less incredulity. We felt, therefore, that the opportunity for studying these little known remains in a region untouched by earlier diggers, was one which should not be neglected; all our subsequent work has accordingly been directed toward the finding and excavation of Basket-maker sites.

In 1915 the junior author regretfully gave up field work in this region to undertake other excavations, and the expeditions of that and the following years were conducted by Mr. Guernsey. The results of 1914 and 1915 have already been published,[2] the present report deals with the explorations of 1916 and 1917; at the close of the latter season field work was temporarily discontinued because of the war. In each year the expeditions were carried on under permits granted by the Secretary of the Interior.

The Museum wishes to make grateful acknowledgment to the following persons whose generous contributions, supplementing the Museum appropriation, served greatly to enlarge the scope of the work: Mrs. S. K. Lothrop, and Messrs. Bronson Cutting, Lawrence Grinnell, F. E. Guernsey, Augustus Hemenway, Henry Horn-

---

[1] Pepper, 1902. The existence of the Basket-makers was first pointed out in print by Dr. T. Mitchell Prudden in *An Elder Brother to the Cliff-dwellers* (Prudden, 1897).

[2] Kidder-Guernsey, 1919.

blower, J. M. Longyear, D. L. Pickman, and John E. Thayer. It wishes also to tender its thanks to Professor Byron Cummings of the University of Arizona, who unselfishly shared with it the field in which he was the pioneer; to Clayton Wetherill for his enthusiastic and faithful services as guide and interpreter; and to Mr. and Mrs. John Wetherill and Mr. Clyde Colville of Kayenta for their unfailing hospitality and constant helpfulness.

In the two seasons covered by this report, the party outfitted at Farmington, New Mexico, and proceeded by wagon and horseback to the trading post of Wetherill and Colville at Kayenta, the base from which further explorations were conducted. Kayenta, which may be found on the more recent Government maps, is reached from Farmington by a journey of four to five days, depending on the condition of the stock, and the abundance of grass and water. The caves and ruins described all lie in Arizona within a radius of one day's ride from Kayenta.

The country exerts a charm which the authors confess their inability to describe. Its physical aspect has already been noted by more competent writers;[1] it is sufficient for the purpose of this paper to say, that although essentially a semi-desert region, there is no difficulty now, nor was there ever, apparently, in earlier times for the dweller here who understood the environment, to obtain sufficient sustenance for simple requirements. The wastes of the valleys and mesa tops that once supplied the wild game with which the early people supplemented the fruits of their agriculture, now furnish ample grazing grounds for the Navajo's flocks of sheep and goats; these Indians also succeed on selected sites in producing good crops of corn, under conditions that to a white farmer would seem quite impossible.

CAMBRIDGE, MASSACHUSETTS
March 5, 1921

[1] Prudden, 1903, pp. 282–285; and 1907; Gregory, 1916, pp. 45–67.

CONTENTS

FIELD WORK, SEASON OF 1916

THE SOUTH COMB

FIELD WORK, SEASON OF 1917

SAYODNEECHEE CANYON

SOUTH COMB REVISITED

SAGIOTSOSI CANYON

MATERIAL CULTURE

FOOD

DRESS AND PERSONAL ORNAMENTS

BASKET-MAKER CAVES OF NORTH-EASTERN ARIZONA

REPORT ON THE EXPLORATIONS OF 1916-17

FIELD WORK, SEASON OF 1916

THE plans of the 1916 expedition included the investigation of a Cliff-dweller ruin discovered the previous year on the west bank of the Chinlee, one day's journey east of Kayenta.[1] A week was spent here. After reprovisioning at Kayenta, camp was made near the mouth of Yellow Head Canyon, about 10 miles to the west, where two days were occupied in examining a small cave and in studying cliff-dwellings that had been cleared by Professor Cummings in 1914. Sunflower Cave (see map, figure 1) a site left unfinished in 1915, was then visited with the object of further investigations.[2] The remainder of the season was occupied in exploring the South Comb and in excavating two caves some 5 miles north of Sunflower Cave.

THE SOUTH COMB [3]

The South Comb is a great sandstone monocline that extends from Marsh Pass in a generally northeastern direction as far as the San Juan River. About 16 miles from Marsh Pass its continuity is broken by a narrow valley which leads through it from Kayenta to the Agathla Rock. Our work was confined to that section lying between the break and Marsh Pass.

Hereabouts the course of the Comb is sinuous and its appearance constantly changing; some stretches are tilted steeply toward the sheer walls of Skeleton Mesa, whose top at those points rises higher than the jagged summit of the Comb itself, which is shown in plate 1, b. Other stretches show gentle inclines that seem to lead to the Mesa, but on reaching the crests the way is invariably blocked by deep intervening chasms. It is hard to imagine more

---

[1] To be described in a separate article.
[2] For the location of this and other sites, see map, figure 1.
[3] For the geology of the region, see Gregory, 1916, p. 47.

1

rugged rock formations than those to be found in this part of the Comb. Frequently, and with little strain on the imagination, one can make out along its crests weird forms in natural sculpture: the outlines of colossal animals, faces, solitary spires and minarets, whose silent grandeur at nightfall intensifies the brooding gloom of

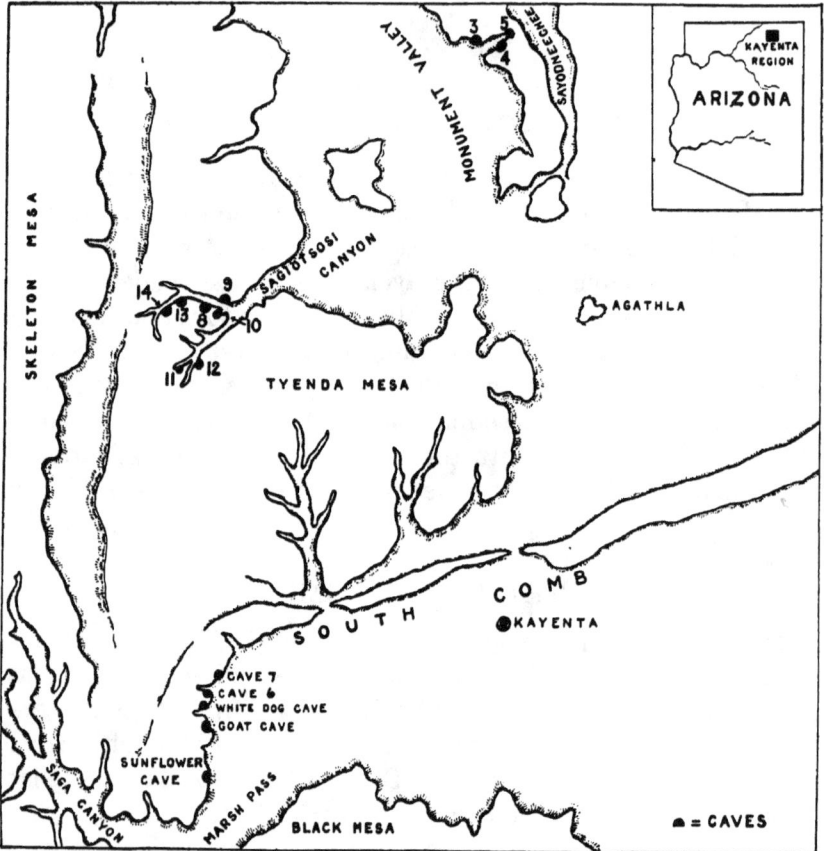

FIGURE 1
Sketch-map of the Kayenta Region.

the desert. In the walls of the tortuous gorges that wind up among the cliffs are countless caves, large and small, many of them so well hidden among the contorted rocks that they can be found only by working one's way on foot along the ledges.

Before exploring for new sites, the expedition occupied itself with two caves found in the Comb during the previous year.

Sunflower Cave Revisited. While work at this site was still in progress in 1915, a sudden flood in Laguna Creek cut off communication between the camp, which lay on the east bank, and the ruin. As time was very limited, it was thought best not to wait the several days that it would probably take for the water to subside; and the party moved on, leaving a section at the rear of the cave unexplored.

Sunflower Cave was occupied by a small cliff-house in which was found the remarkable cache of ceremonial objects that gave the place its name.[1] Of even greater interest, however, was the presence of certain remains which led us to suspect that in this cave might be found evidence as to the relative age of the Basket-maker and Cliff-dweller cultures. Cist 4, sunk into the hard-pan behind the cliff-house rooms, had given the most positive indications of this; it is described as follows in the previous report (p. 96):

> The outlines of this cist could be traced by a disturbed area showing in the face of the trench. It had originally been a stone enclosure, though but two of the slabs were still in place. A few bones of a child were found in the upper part; near the bottom at the side nearest the back of the cave were two decorated bone tubes. Imprints of coiled basketry could be seen in hard lumps of the adobe filling, but nothing of the basket itself remained. The cist gave us the impression that it had been a Basket-maker burial chamber which had been pulled to pieces, partly emptied and then filled in with rubbish during the cliff-house period.

There was also found in the loose rubbish a typical Basket-maker sandal, the presence of which, in what was a purely cliff-house site to all outward appearance, required some explanation.

We were accordingly very anxious to examine the still undug portions at the rear of the cave. The results of the second visit amply repaid the effort, for we discovered unmistakable stratigraphic evidence of a sequence of occupation. The new excavations revealed Basket-maker burials, some of them entirely undisturbed, below a stratum of typical Cliff-dweller débris. The location of the finds is shown on the plan (figure 2); their relation to the Cliff-dweller remains is clearly brought out in the diagrammatic cross-section (figure 3).

Cist 5 (cists 1 to 4 opened in 1915) was a shallow bowl-shaped hole dug in the hard-pan. In it were parts of the skeletons of a young

[1] For a general description of this cave and of the finds made there in 1915, see Kidder-Guernsey, 1919, pp. 92–96.

child and an adult, while scattered through the loose dirt about the top were portions of the skeleton of a second child, which had probably originally been deposited with the other remains.   The bones

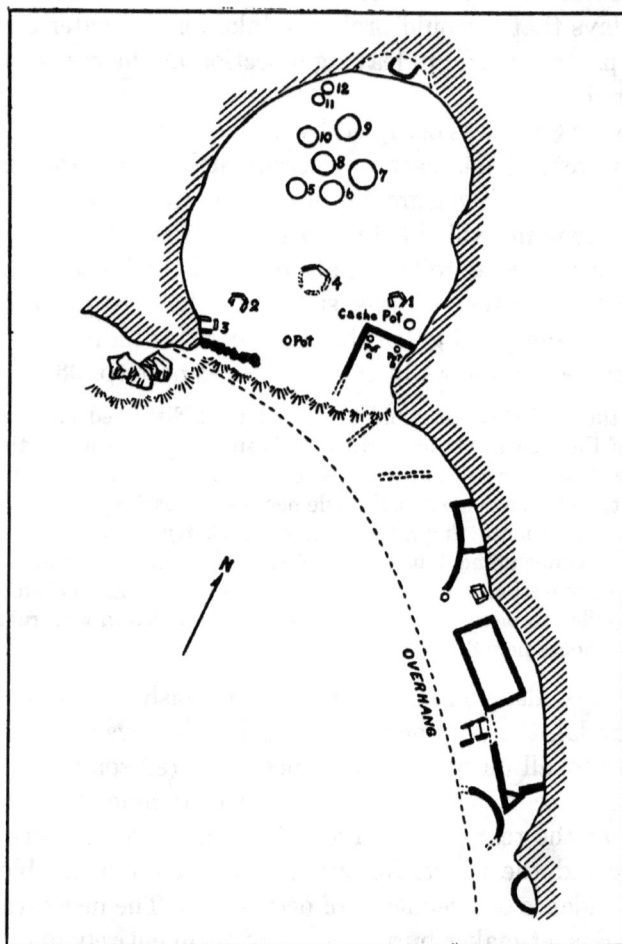

FIGURE 2
Plan of Sunflower Cave, South Comb.

of the adult had been carefully disposed at the bottom of the hole, in a manner to make the most of the limited space. They consisted of an undeformed skull in good preservation, the long bones of the arms, the scapulae, and a few ribs and vertebrae. The arm bones were placed on either side of the skull, the other bones being packed close about it. Lying across the arm bones was a section of a femur which showed a long splintered post-mortem break. The lower jaw was found in the loose rubbish some fifteen inches from the edge of the cist.

It had probably been dragged out by rats, a thing we found to be not uncommon in caves. A small white chipped point lay among the bones. Above these remains was the disarranged skeleton of the young child. The second child's skeleton as before stated, was scattered through the loose earth about the cist. We

FIGURE 3
Sunflower Cave, Cross-section.

are at a loss to account for the neat arrangement of the adult bones. It is clearly a case of secondary burial, but we have never found any instance of this practice in undisturbed Basket-maker sites, and the people who looted Basket-maker graves did not, as far as we are aware, ever trouble themselves to restore anything to place.

Cist 6 was 2 feet 6 inches in diameter and was cut 3 feet deep into the hard-pan. It lay 4 feet east of Cist 5, and contained only a quantity of loose cedar bark and shredded grass piled in the bottom. It is possible that the bones found in Cist 5 came from here, though no positive evidence remained that it had been used for burial.

Cist 7 was an untouched Basket-maker grave; the original filling passed unbroken above it, and was in turn overlaid by Cliff-dweller rubbish (figure 3). It was 4 feet in diameter, 3 feet deep, and held the well-preserved skeletons of two adults with undeformed crania. They lay flexed on their left sides, hands between the lower thighs (plate 10, c); over the head of each was inverted a small coiled basket, one of which can be seen in the photograph. The

5

earth about the skeletons showed traces of decayed organic matter, probably from fur-string robes and other wrappings; rotted cedar bark was found at the bottom. The only object besides the decomposed baskets was a small strip of bark with one end neatly trimmed off.

Cists 8, 9 and 10 had all been plundered in early times and contained only fragmentary skeletons; a number of cylindrical seed beads accompanied the remains of a child in Cist 10.

Cists 11 and 12 were within 3 feet of the rear wall of the cave. Although very close under the surface they had not been molested. Cist 11 was a shallow bowl-shaped scoop in the hard-pan, and held two infants. One of these had been wrapped in a fur-string blanket and lay on what seemed to be a twined-woven cedar-bark mat, beneath which was a reed-backed cradle too badly rotted to preserve. Infant 2 was also wrapped in a fur-string blanket and lay on a decayed reed-backed cradle; near the head were remains of a coiled basket inverted over traces of a substance resembling meal. Both cradles were of the rigid type shown in plate 20. Accompanying the bodies were two bark objects covered with prairie-dog skin, which we have since been able to identify as umbilical pads. Cist 12 was a small hole in the hard-pan. In it was an infant wrapped in a fur-string robe and encased in a twined-woven bag. The robe had been destroyed by insects, but the bag was in a fair state of preservation.

All the above Basket-maker cists lay below a layer of cliff-house rubbish from 6 to 8 inches deep, made up of ashes, turkey droppings, bits of straw and many potsherds of the same wares as those found on other cliff-house sites in this region. Beneath this rubbish, the surface of the hard-pan above the cists gave no indication of their presence, being as compact and of the same appearance as the surrounding hard-pan. If, therefore, we had followed the 1915 method of clearing and examining the Cliff-dweller rubbish down to the hard-pan, and not cutting into it except where the tops of cists were encountered or other surface indications excited interest, these burials would have escaped notice altogether.

Fortunately, however, the trench was run much deeper than usual and entered Cist 7 from the side. The section thus exposed showed the top to be filled to a depth of 1 foot with a compactly tamped mass exactly like the hard-pan in which the cist itself was

SOUTH COMB
a, White Dog Cliff and Navajo Hogan; b, South Comb, near White Dog Cave.

excavated (figure 3). That the infant burials in Cists 11 and 12 remained undiscovered through the period of Cliff-dweller occupancy is remarkable, since they were covered by hardly more than 3 inches of the cave earth; the Cliff-dweller rubbish here was also very thin. A possible explanation may be that this part of the cave was used by the Cliff-dwellers for storage or for sleeping places, and was thus in a measure protected from the random digging to which the more open portions were exposed.

Had the Cliff-dwellers, the final tenants of the cave, been more persistent in their search, there would have remained no trace of the Basket-maker period except the cists, empty or refilled with Cliff-dweller rubbish. Attention is called to this for the sake of emphasis, as further on in this report, caves are described where all evidence of Basket-maker occupancy other than the empty cists has been effaced.

Goat Cave. This site was located by the expedition of 1915. It lies about two miles north of Sunflower Cave at the foot of a steep incline leading to the top of the Comb (see figure 1). The approach is through a narrow ravine choked with great rocks, among which a thick growth of large old cedars has found root. These trees screen the place from view except at a few points in the ravine. The cave is a deep shelter at the west end of which is an even deeper recess. As shown in the plan (figure 4) there are two levels: a front or lower one, extending the entire length of the cave; and a higher rear level, consisting of the whole floor of the inner recess and of a narrow gallery running all along the back of the more open part of the cave. The whole upper level is formed of the original hard-pan fill; along the gallery or terrace this breaks away in a vertical bank. The walls and roof of the cave are much blackened by smoke. At one point in the rear of the cave the floor is covered by a thick layer of ashes and charcoal. In the recess and on the end of the gallery next to it, are a number of partly fallen walls (plate 2, a, b).

Room 1, five feet in diameter, the walls 2 feet 4 inches high, is built of upright slabs of stone.

Room 2, from the foundations that remain, appears to have been oval in shape. From front to back it measured 8 feet, its length could not be determined as the end wall had disappeared. The foundation is of thick stone slabs of uniform size set on end, on these small stones were laid flat (plate 2, *a*), but little of the upper course remained in place. Joints between the foundation slabs were closed with adobe mortar. The upper courses appear to have been chinked with the same material. Back of this room are remains of two curved walls built of coursed masonry in the usual Cliff-dweller manner. Stone apparently from these walls was used to construct a small cairn on the opposite side of the recess. It

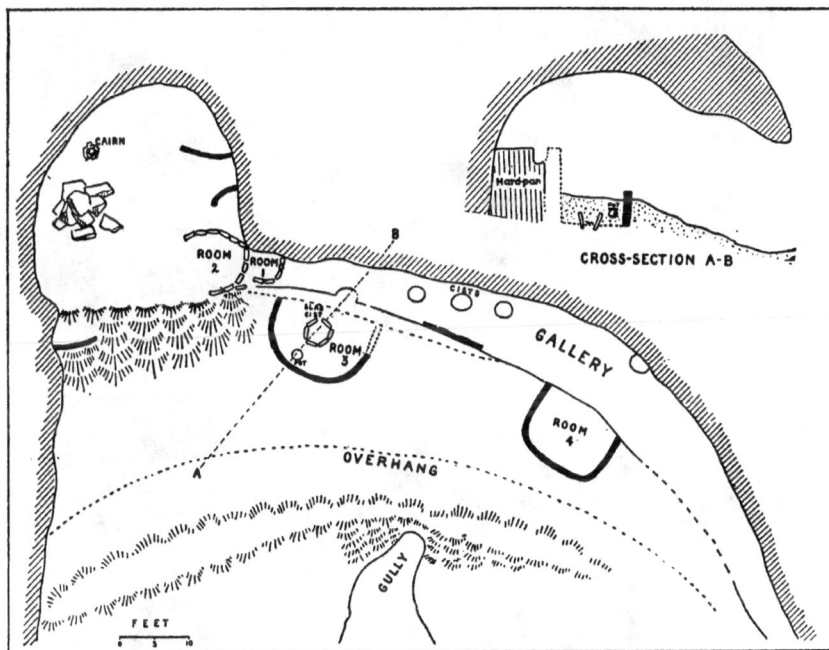

FIGURE 4
Plan and Cross-section of Goat Cave, South Comb.

resembles monuments built by the Navajo to mark water or trails; nothing was found beneath it. Directly in front of the cairn is a heap of rocks fallen from the roof of the cave.

On the lower level in front of the gallery are two roughly circular rooms which we at first wrongly thought to be Cliff-dweller kivas, but they were found to contain none of the special features of ceremonial rooms. Both were built against the steep bank of the terrace which had been cut away to form their rear walls.

Room 3, the less well-preserved of the two, measured 15 feet across its greatest diameter; the wall stood 4 feet at its highest

GOAT CAVE

a, Slab foundation of Room 2; b, General view, Room 3 in foreground.

point. The masonry is interesting and unusual; medium-sized flat stones are laid up without any mortar in such a way as to produce an even surface on the interior (plate 2, b), the exterior being left irregular and rough. So carefully are the stones placed that in spite of the absence of mortar the construction is firm and solid. In clearing this room a slab cist was uncovered, measuring 4 feet in diameter at the top, 3 feet at the bottom, and 2 feet deep; in the bottom was a 2-inch layer of ashes and charcoal and over this 2 inches of cedar bark. It was very similar to Basket-maker slab cists found in Cave 1, 1915.[1] The original floor of Room 3 was so ill-defined that we could not determine exactly the relation of the cist to the floor, but as near as could be judged the upright slabs had been sunk into it a depth of about 8 inches.

Cached in the loose filling of the room, at the point indicated in the plan (figure 4; note also its position in the cross-section) was a black corrugated olla. It was covered with a thin flat stone, but contained only drift sand.

Room 4. The general shape of this room is shown in the plan. Its greatest diameter, measured inside, is fourteen feet, from back to front eleven feet. The highest point in the wall, five feet, is probably the original height, as no loose building stones were noticed here. No trace of roofing remains. The masonry wall has no sharp corners. The back wall is cut in the face of the gallery and has a slight bend or angle. The stones are laid to produce a smooth face on the inside as in Room 3, and with considerable skill, since they are still firmly in place though there is no trace of adobe mortar in the joints. In excavating the room we found quantities of charcoal and scattered bundles of cedar bark, but no artifacts. Two rude cists lined with cedar bark were also opened. As in Room 3 the floor was not well-defined.

In the floor of the gallery were several jar-shaped cists dug in the hard-pan (see figure 4). These were exactly like the burial cists found in the Sayodneechee burial cave, 1914.[2] At a point back of Room 3 where the terrace wall had caved off carrying with it one half a cist (see section in figure 4) the exposed cross-section showed plainly the marks of digging sticks in the side of the cist thus brought to view. Two of the cists contained a few human bones;

[1] Kidder-Guernsey, 1919, p. 77 and plate 27.
[2] Ibid., p. 28 and figure 8.

while other portions of skeletons, some bleached by long exposure, were found in the loose sand covering the floor of the terrace. These were, no doubt, plundered Basket-maker burials.

The authors wish to call particular attention to the rooms uncovered in this cave. Their masonry, with the exception of the single wall in the recess, is quite different from that of the cliff-dwellings.

White Dog Cave. This was by far the most prolific site discovered by the Museum's expeditions to northeastern Arizona. Its position is most inconspicuous and the first view of it was obtained during a climb high up among the rocks of the Comb, the only place in fact, from which it could be seen from any distance. It might easily have escaped notice altogether, for a rider passing along the valley below would not be tempted to explore the narrow ravine leading up to it, particularly as the cliff in which it is located is apparently in full view and seems to be entirely unbroken (see plate 1, a). One short section of the cliff is, however, out of sight from the flat land, and just there is tucked away the cave. The above conditions are described thus at length in order to show the absolute necessity of a careful search *on foot* among all the little side canyons of this broken country.

The approach is up a tortuous ravine. Arriving below it the visitor is astonished that so great a cavern should be so effectively hidden. It occupies a commanding position in the rounded front of a buttress-like swell of the cliff. The huge portal, 120 feet across the base and at least 125 feet high, seems carved by nature to conform to the dome-shaped top of the cliff above it. The accompanying photograph (plate 3), aside from having in it no familiar objects by which relative proportions may be judged, shows so clearly the process of formation and general aspect that further description is unnecessary.

Reaching the cave after a stiff climb of 100 feet up a steep talus, one enters a spacious chamber measuring approximately 70 feet from back wall to line of shelter and 120 feet across the opening. The ceiling is high and arched, the floor rises at an easy grade from front to back. Somewhat more than half the floor space is covered by large rocks fallen from the roof, one of which measures 20 feet in length, 12 feet in width and 10 feet thick (figure 5 and plate 11, a). This and other rocks near it we found later had fallen since the

WHITE DOG CAVE.

cave was occupied. The unencumbered portion of the floor was composed of clean sand and small broken stones. Although we subsequently unearthed considerable accumulations of ashes and charcoal in different parts of the cave, the walls and ceilings showed not a trace of soot, having been scoured clean by wind-blown sand. A demonstration of this process was furnished one day when a high wind from the proper quarter created a veritable

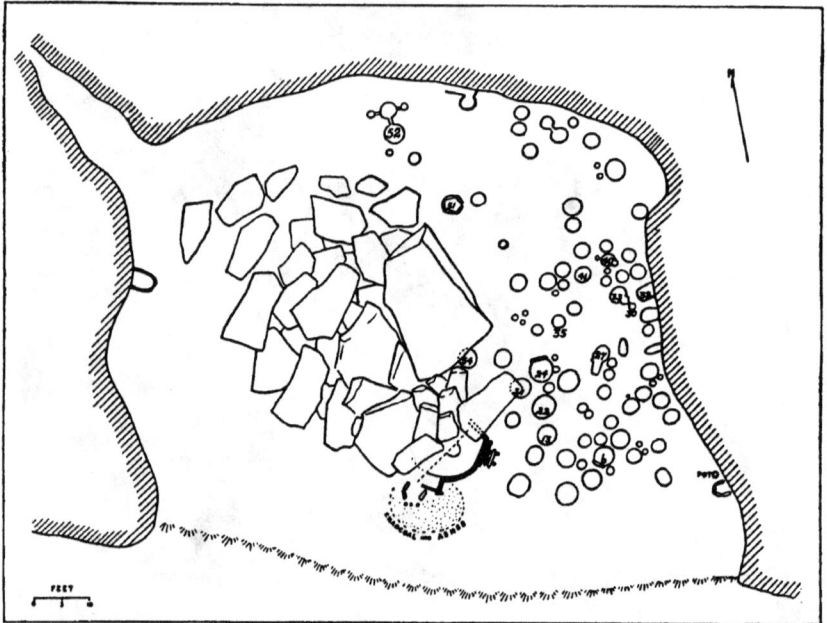

FIGURE 5

Plan of White Dog Cave, South Comb.

whirlwind in the cave, gathering up the surface sand and swirling it about in such quantities that we were forced to abandon work while it continued. A piece of paper released at the back would sometimes make as many as three complete circuits of the cave clinging close to the wall except as it passed across the front. On mentioning this to Mrs. Wetherill we were told by her that the place was known to the Navajo as the Cave of Winds.

The first examination of the cave for traces of occupation showed at the back against the wall the tops of several sand-filled cists, dug in the hard-pan. Searching the surface, a few bleached human bones were seen and a small handful of Cliff-dweller pot-sherds was picked up. Digging at random with a trowel, a few fragments of basketry and some bone beads were found. Near the center of the cave the ends of two upright stakes were noticed, projecting from 2 to 3 inches above the surface. Not until our second and more thorough examination did we discover on the west side a low foundation wall mudded on to the sloping rock floor of the cave. This was apparently the beginning of a small Cliff-dweller storage room or bin. As a "prospect" the cave fulfilled every requirement. Its exploration yielded a collection which fully represents most phases of the material culture of the Basket-makers.

Across the front of the cave where work was commenced there was found a natural ridge of coarse débris, back of which the sand fill had accumulated above the hard-pan floor to a depth of from 5 to 7 feet. Toward the back this deposit grew shallower until along the rear wall the hard-pan cropped to the surface.

The fill carried no refuse pockets or well-defined rubbish layers such as are found marking floor levels in Cliff-dweller caves. In general it was made up of a surface layer 6 inches to 1 foot deep of drift sand, below which it was composed of sand and bits of stone mixed with straw, pieces of bark, and particles of charcoal.

Occasionally there appeared thin strata of coarse charcoal and in certain areas there were encountered quite extensive accumulations of ashes and charcoal. In the general digging a number of specimens were found at various depths. They consisted mainly of basket sherds, fragments of fur-string blankets and tattered bits of woven bags; a mummified foot and other fragments of human remains were also recovered. All other objects were taken from cists.

In the plan, figure 5, are indicated a large number of cists grouped along the east wall; there were no cists on the west and north sides. The majority of these were jar-shaped excavations in the hard-pan ranging in size from small pot-holes 1 foot in diameter and of about the same depth, to examples 5 feet deep and 4 feet 6 inches in diameter. Some burials were found in this type of cist but for the most part they were empty, save for sand or sometimes cedar bark and grass at the bottom. Most of the burials were in the front half of the cist area. A few, as was just stated, were in

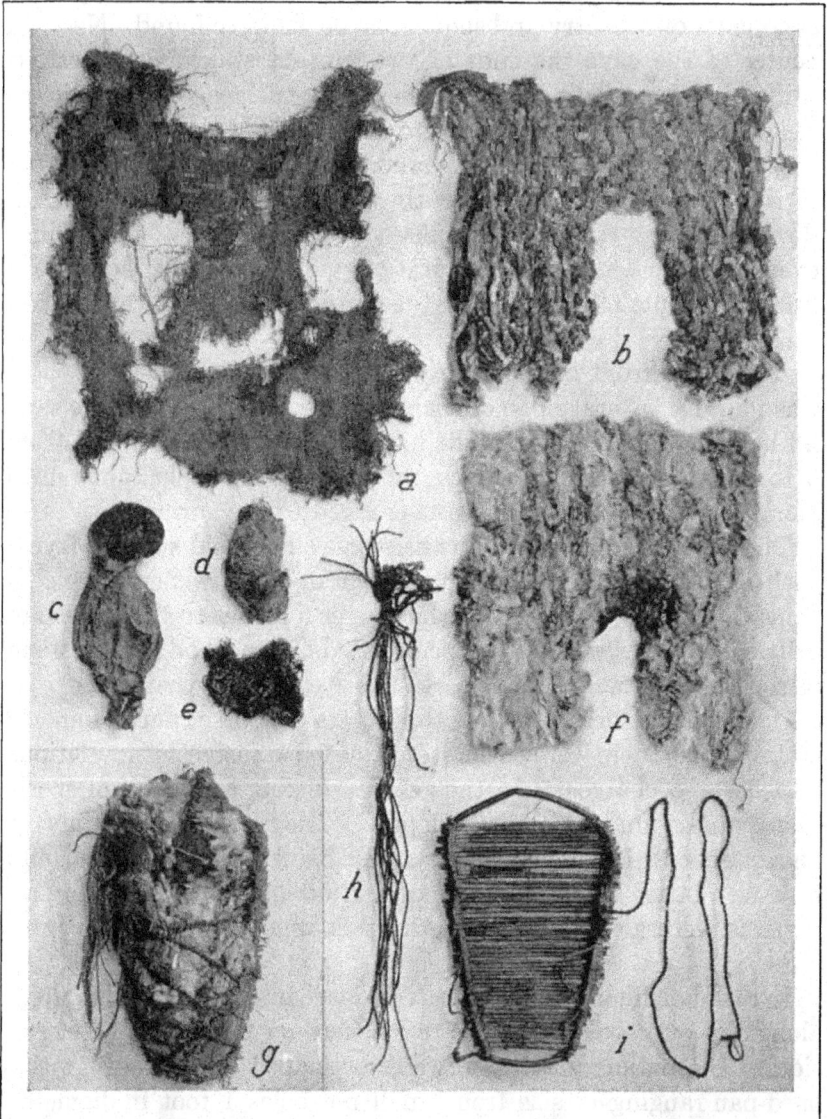

WHITE DOG CAVE

g, Cradle bundle as found. The other figures show cradle and contents unwrapped.
a, Woven cloth; b, f, Fur cloth blankets; c, Mummy of child; d, Umbilical pad;
e, Absorbent bark; i, Cradle. (About 1/12.)

cists completely excavated in the hard-pan, others were in shallow excavations in the hard-pan with one or two stone slabs so placed as to hold back the loose sand, and a single burial was in a cist (51) of the stone slab type described in the previous report.[1] Some of the burials had been previously disturbed,[2] but a number were found intact, the remains and mortuary offerings in a remarkably fine state of preservation.

In the account of the excavations which follows, certain cists and burials are described in detail. The intention is to present the salient features of the more typical ones, hence many small objects found in the cists or concealed among the wrappings of the mummies are not enumerated. They are, however, described in detail in another section.

Cist 6 (figure 6, a). The first burial cist to be encountered measured 3 feet in diameter, 2 feet in depth and was 4 feet below the surface. It represents a type that was evidently constructed primarily for sepulchre. At one side was an upright stone slab. Although the cist had been relieved of a good portion of its contents by ancient diggers we obtained from it a collection which required 51 catalogue numbers to record. In the upper part were the scattered bones of three infants; at the bottom a few bones from the skeleton of an adult. In the loose fill were several bunches of human hair (plate 32, c, d). A quantity of human hair evidently from the head of a mummy[3] that had been pulled from the cist was also found in the loose fill. One small strand was wrapped about with a leather thong. Later we found in another cist a mummy with coiffure intact, having a queue-like strand wrapped in the same manner. These were practically all the human remains that were left. At the bottom against one side were a quantity of piñon nuts, the rotted remains of woven bags, loose beads, basket sherds, pieces of woven bags and fur-string robes.

Cist 13, a shallow bowl-shaped excavation, contained the remains of two infants. One, a very young child wrapped in two fur-string blankets and a fragment of woven cloth, was lashed

---

[1] Kidder-Guernsey, 1919, p. 77 and plate 27.

[2] This grave looting so commonly found in Basket-maker cave cemeteries is not modern. Although we have no direct evidence in its support, our theory is that it was the work of the Cliff-dwellers. See Kidder-Guernsey, 1919, p. 84.

[3] The mummies were, of course, not artificially preserved in any way; they are merely desiccated bodies.

tightly to a small reed-backed cradle; an umbilical pad was in place and the dried umbilical cord was tied to one of the blankets. This mummy bundle as found, and also unwrapped so that all its parts can be seen, is shown in plate 4. The second body, that of a child about 4 years of age, was completely encased in a woven bag [1] (plate 30, f). It was also shrouded in a fur-string robe. Beneath this bundle were pieces of a cedar-bark mat, and over it was spread a fur-string blanket (plate 16, a) which was in turn covered by an

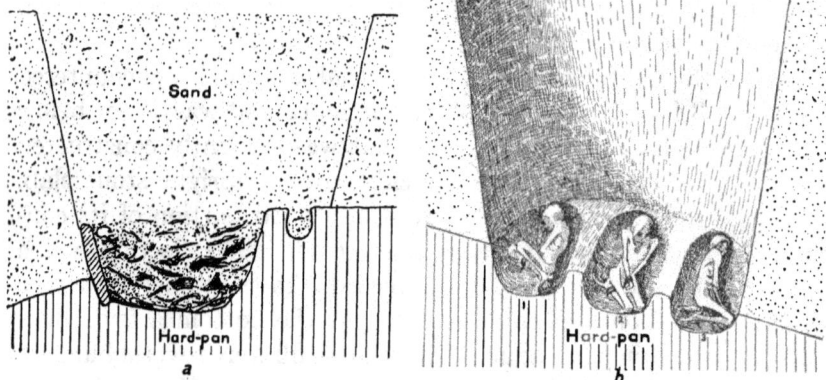

FIGURE 6

White Dog Cave: a, Cross-section of Cist 6; b, Cross-section of Cist 22.

inverted tray basket. At one side of the cist was a bowl-shaped basket also inverted. In the fill some 8 inches above the tray basket was a skin bag containing shelled corn (plate 15). At one side of the cist lay an atlatl in perfect condition save that before being placed in the cist it had been bent nearly double. This and the baskets are illustrated *in situ* in plate 10, e.

Cist 22 contained the bodies of three individuals. Its shape was roughly circular, the greatest diameter being 5 feet 2 inches, depth 2 feet 10 inches; the top was 5 feet 6 inches below the surface. Each body occupied a shallow depression scooped out of the bottom of the cist as shown in figure 6, b. The remains were partly mummified though not in a good state of preservation. The heads,

[1] The design on this bag is shown in color in plate 28.

however, retained their hair and much of the dried tissue of the face. Each body had been wrapped in a fur-string blanket and sewed up in woven bags, all of which were in an advanced state of decay.

Number 1, the body of a young female, lay on its right side, knees drawn up and hands between the thighs. A skein-like rope of human hair was wound around the left forearm, passed between the thighs and made fast about the right leg below the knee. At the waist were fragments of a string apron. Some portions of bags that had been used to cover the body remained. A fragment at the feet was of very fine weave while pieces adhering to the knees were much coarser. Covering the whole were two tray baskets. Number 2 was a female. Three baskets were used to cover the body. It rested on its back with head and legs inclined to the left; the feet were drawn up close to the body; the upper legs, bent at the hips, were at right angles to the torso. The hands were in front of the lap, and were bound together at the wrists by fourteen turns of a tightly twisted cord of human hair. This cord was then knotted to a skein-like rope of human hair and both rope and cord passed through between the thighs and about the lower legs above the ankles. At the waist were remains of a string apron and on the breast lay a disk-shaped pendant of shell, ornamented with incised lines. About the neck were beads of olivella shells and thin disk-beads cut from shell, together with part of the leather string by which they had been suspended. In the bottom of the cist under the body were a number of dice-like stones and a single corn cob. Number 3 (male, 20 to 25 years of age) rested on its left side, limbs loosely flexed, hands between thighs. Two tray baskets covered the body. At the right side lay a grooved club, at the feet were a pair of badly rotted square-toed sandals with leather tie-strings and a quantity of small deer or antelope hoofs. Near the hoofs were two handle-like bone objects with small stones attached to their ends. About the neck was a string of shell beads. Among the objects found under the body was a fine chipped knife blade (plate 35, k) and its shrunken wooden haft.

Cist 24 held the mummies of two adults, one male and one female, each accompanied by the remains of a dog, and an unusual number of mortuary offerings. The remarkably fine state of preservation of everything in this cist is due to the fact that the burials were surrounded by dry sand. The excavation in the hard-pan made to receive the bodies was a shallow hole just deep enough to hold them. As in Cist 22, each individual occupied a scooped-out place in the bottom of the cist. At the back was an upright stone slab; as none were used at the front or sides, its purpose was evidently to hold back the loose sand while the hard-pan was being excavated. Just in front of the slab was a stout log 3 feet in length, the ends and sides charred by fire. This reached to the surface and was one of the stakes observed when the cave was entered (see upper right center, plate 6, a); whether or not it was so placed at the time the burials were made we were unable to tell. It may have been a marker, but we have found no other burials indicated in this way.

Mummy 1 (female) lay on its right side, limbs loosely flexed. Two large woven bags split down the side encased the remains, one drawn over the head, the other over the feet; the tops met at the middle of the body and were sewn together with yucca leaves (plate 7, a). As usual the corpse was wrapped in a fur-string robe. Over it were inverted two baskets, a bowl-shaped one covering the feet; the other a large carrying basket with tump-line attached covering the head and upper part of the body. The baskets and the manner in which a number of digging sticks were disposed in the grave is shown in plate 6, a. The planting stick at the front with one end resting on the edge of the cist was evidently placed to hold the basket upright. The cedar bark that appears in the upper left hand corner is from another cist. On removing the carrying basket, a small dog was found lying below it on the left side of the mummy. Under the bowl-shaped basket was a substance resembling meal. On lifting the body from the cist there was found beneath it a thick bed of fur and feathers compacted by decay into a mass that was taken out unbroken. On examination at the Museum this proved to have embedded in it bundles of feathers, skin containers and skin bags; these and their contents are described under Material Culture. On the bottom of the cist was a badly shrunken, but complete atlatl and near it, but not in contact with it, was a roughly chipped piece of quartzite which may originally have been tied to its back. At one side on the bottom was a wand with a yucca braid and twigs attached to one end. Quantities of grass seed, piñon nuts and squash seeds were also found at the bottom of the cist.

a, Cradle *in situ*, Cist 54, White Dog Cave; b, Cave 10, Sagiotsosi Canyon.

Mummy 2 (male about 35 years of age) lay on its left side with feet drawn up tight against the body; head east and facing south. It was wrapped in the same manner as mummy 1 (see plate 8). Inverted over the body was a large pannier basket which is shown behind the front basket in the photograph (plate 6, a); over the head was a bowl-shaped basket. A second basket of the same shape lay just to one side, covering the fragments of a squash shell vessel. Removing the pannier, three tray-shaped baskets graduated in size with the smallest at the bottom were found beneath. The pannier also partly covered the remains of a large long haired and nearly white dog, which in turn lay across the two bowl-shaped baskets (see plate 6, b). There was also found under the pannier a large quantity of flies, the dog having apparently been already fly blown when placed in the cist. The eggs evidently hatched and the flies died in the space under the carrying basket without ever seeing the light of day. We thought that the flies might serve to fix the time of year in which these burials were made, but Mr. N. Banks of the Museum of Comparative Zoölogy, to whom we are indebted for their identification, informs us that they are *Caliphora coloradensis*, a very hardy species which flourishes from early spring to late fall, so it is not possible to fix a very definite date by them. The digging sticks might indicate that the spring planting was in progress, but this is of course mere conjecture.

Extending from the edge of this cist on the east side was a shallow hole just deep enough and of sufficient size to contain the remains of a young infant. Only the bones, and part of a badly rotted fur-string robe were left.

Cist 27. The unusual plan of this cist is shown in figure 5. It was dug in hard-pan to a depth of 2 feet 10 inches, measured 4 feet 9 inches in length and 2 feet 6 inches at its widest point. The sand and fill above had a depth of about 1 foot. One side of the cist was formed by the face of a vertical break in the rock floor of the cave, the ledge nearly cropping through the hard-pan at this point, a circumstance which probably accounts for the elongated shape, as the rounded end seems to indicate an original intention to dig the conventional circular cist. In it were found the partly mummified bodies of two adults placed one above the other, facing in opposite directions (plate 9, a).

Number 1, the uppermost, an adult, probably male, lay face down, knees drawn up and crushed against the chest, feet under hips, left arm extended at full length along the side; the right forearm was bent across the waist. Number 2, a male of about 25 years, lay on the bottom of the cist directly under mummy 1 and with head in the opposite direction. The limbs were arranged in practically the same manner as those of the upper mummy, the feet of which rested on the face of this one.

Accompanying these remains was a large number of specimens some in a good state of preservation, though objects at the bottom of the cist and baskets at the top and sides had suffered from decay. We were, however, able to determine that there had been at least seven baskets, mostly medium sized trays. In preparing the cist to receive the bodies, a number of atlatl spear-shafts had been broken into various lengths and placed crisscross on the bottom. On the upper side a few inches out from the rock there stood on edge a rectangular frame of sunflower stalks and broken atlatl spear-shafts tied at right angles to each other. Back of it, also on edge, were placed several tray baskets. On the opposite side next to mummy 2 were bundles of sticks or reeds so badly shrunken that their nature could not be made out with certainty; they were probably atlatl spear-shafts. Placed over mummy 2 were more spear-shafts and the bundled fragments of a wooden device, part of which is figured in plate 36, d, e. At one side of mummy 1 were two grooved clubs. Quantities of grass and squash seed were found in much decayed skin containers; also a number of small objects, among them a fine chipped knife blade, beads of seed and stone, pendants of shell and stone, a comb-like head-ornament and a bone handle with leather strings attached.

Cist 30 was a jar-shaped excavation in the hard-pan, 15 inches in diameter at the top, 23 inches in diameter, 1 foot below the rim, and 24 inches in depth. In it were the skeletons of six infants. Four were found in woven bags. Of other wrappings there remained tattered pieces of dressed skin and bits of fur-string. Five umbilical pads, similar to those from Cist 11, Sunflower Cave, were taken from various parts of this cist. These could not be assigned to individual burials as the skeletons were more or less mixed as if the cist had been partly rifled in early times. At the bottom were two cradles in excellent condition. A few inches

WHITE DOG CAVE

a, Cist 24, partly cleared, showing baskets *in situ*; b, Pannier baskets removed, showing small baskets, mummy of white dog, and many dead flies.

above these were about 8 quarts of shelled corn; no trace of a container could be found. Scattered through the fill were beads of seed, stone, and olivella shell, a green stone pendant, a small grinding stone, and two strips of bark, like the piece found in Cist 7, Sunflower Cave. Joined to this cist by a small funnel-like hole was a second cist, the same diameter but not so deep, while cutting the rim of this was a third and larger one (Cist 33, figure 5). These were empty; they form a good example of a number of similar arrangements found in the course of the excavation (see Cist 52, figure 5). All are characterized by one or more small flue-like holes dug down from the surface and penetrating the sides of the cist, or, as in the case above noted, connecting small potholes to the cist (plate 9, d, and plate 14, a). Sometimes these holes, instead of entering the large cist obliquely, were dug at nearly right angles from the pothole to the side of the larger cist. As a rule cists of this type were empty save for bark or grass stalks. They strikingly resemble the field pit-ovens used by the Hopi for roasting corn;[1] there are no indications, however, that these had ever had fires built in them.

Cist 31 as shown in the plan, figure 5, was partly under one end of a large rock. In order to reach it we were obliged to remove from the surface many others, some so large that they had first to be broken up. The top of the cist was 3 feet 6 inches below the surface, its greatest diameter 4 feet, depth 1 foot 10 inches. At one side was a single stone slab. In the cist was the partly mummi-fied body of an adult, the bones of the skeleton held together by dried tissue and caked adobe (plate 7, b). The remains rested on the left side, knees drawn up level with chin, hands palms to-gether under left cheek and supporting head. A woven bag cov-ered the head and shoulders. It had been split down the side before drawing on, then sewn together again with yucca leaves. A portion of the bag was in good condition. Over the mouth of the mummy outside the bag, was tied a sandal of the square-toed type. About the feet and lower part of the body were the remains of a fur-string blanket. The bag and wrappings were held in place by a binding of yucca leaves. About the neck were seed beads. Inverted over the middle of the body was a coarse bowl-shaped basket; under it lay a quantity of plant stalks, apparently

[1] Hough, 1919, figure 3.

of Brigham tea, also an animal bone and a pointed twig with a string attached. In the lap, as shown in plate 7, b, was a bundle made up of two wooden implements, a foreshaft with stone point, a wand-like stick with a bunch of reddish fiber tied to the end, and a small woven object, the whole wrapped about with a feather headdress and a number of turns of fine string (plate 40). The fill about the body was caked and discolored. Nothing was found in the cist under the body.

Cist 32 gave indications of previous disturbance. It was dug in the hard-pan against the side of the cave and showed more than usual care in the smoothing of its walls. It was oval in shape, 3 feet 6 inches in length, 2 feet in width, and 2 feet 6 inches deep. In the edge of the end opposite the cave wall was a shallow groove perhaps made to seat a cover. In the upper part of the cist was the skeleton of an infant and remains of a small reed-backed cradle, both too far gone to collect. In a sub-excavation at the bottom was the skeleton of a child about six years of age, knees drawn up to chin, head north, face southeast. About the remains were traces of fur-string wrappings and coiled basketry; under them a small quantity of green powder. This cist was probably originally a storage cist and perhaps had a stone slab cover which fitted into the groove at the end. It may have contained at one time other remains than those found, for it would hardly have been dug for them alone, as it was of much greater size than necessary.

Cist 35 was not dug straight into the hard-pan, but was slightly undercut. It measured 1 foot 3 inches across at the top and 2 feet 6 inches in greatest diameter; the bottom was rounded. In it was the mummy of a baby on a reed-backed cradle; the body was enclosed in a bag and lay on a twined-woven cedar-bark mat (plate 21, d). All were in good condition. The mat appears to be part of an old cedar-bark cradle like the ones found in Caves 1 and 2 by the 1915 expedition.[1]

Cist 40 was a large jar-shaped storage cist excavated in the hard-pan. It was very symmetrical in shape and measured 2 feet in diameter at the top, 4 feet in diameter 2 feet below the rim, and 4 feet 6 inches in depth (plate 9, b). The rim was 2 feet below the surface. In the top was found a rabbit net tied in a compact bundle, together with a quantity of apocynum bark done up in

---

[1] Kidder-Guernsey, 1915, p. 165 and plate 72.

26

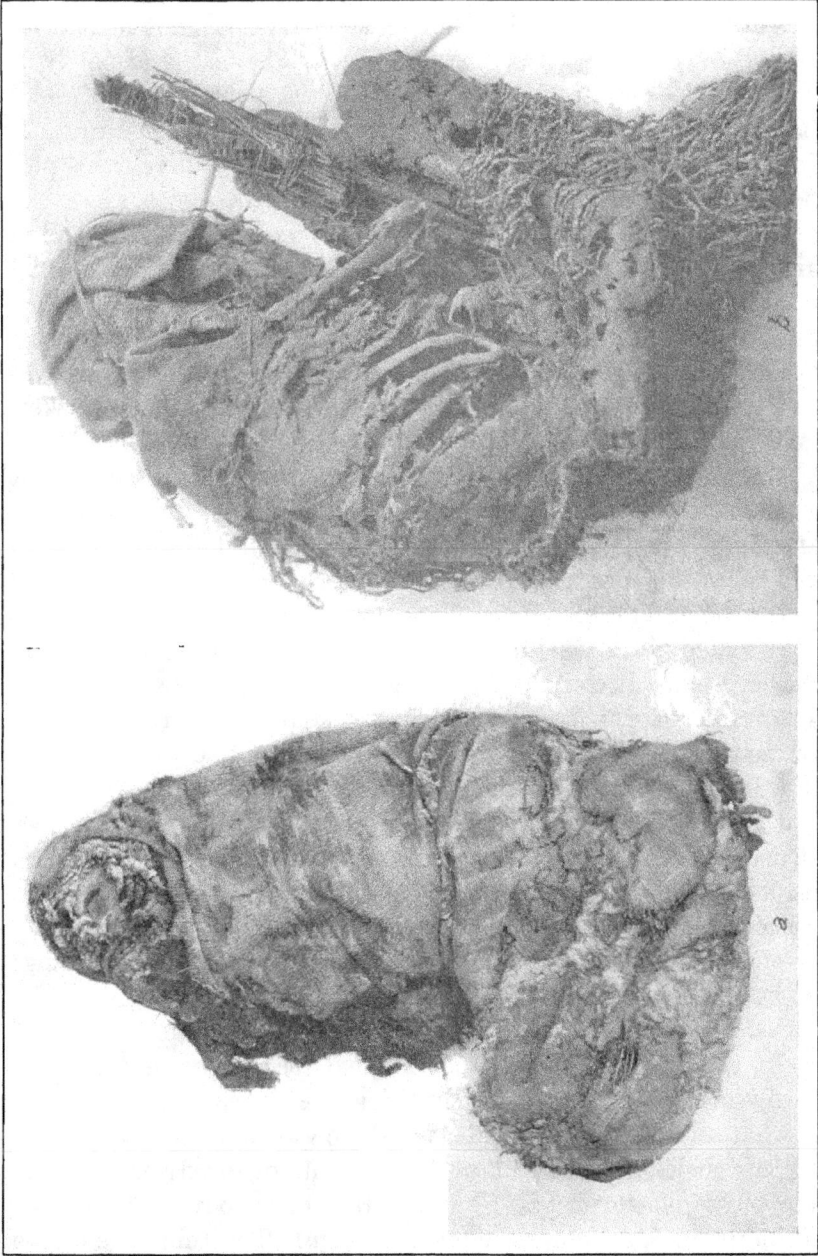

White Dog Cave

a, Wrapped mummy of woman from Cist 24: b, Mummy of man from Cist 31.

bundles. The net had evidently been cached here after the cist was abandoned and filled up, since the hole in which it rested was partly dug in the hard-pan at the edge of the cist, and partly in the fill of the cist itself. In clearing the cist a thick layer of cedar bark was found 1 foot from the bottom; below it was clean sand. One foot from the rim on the side opposite the net there was a pot-hole, 1 foot in diameter and the same in depth.

The rabbit net, a remarkable specimen, is described in detail in another place. Its lack of definite relation to the cist or to other Basket-maker remains at first raised a doubt in the authors' minds as to whether it might not have belonged to a later period. On the other hand it will be remembered that a very similar excavation at the side of Cist 24 contained the remains of a Basket-maker infant.

Cist 41 gave evidence of previous disturbance. On clearing it a small niche was found in one side that contained the remains of an infant, a small basket, a skin covered object (umbilical pad) and the usual fur-string robe.

Cist 51, 3 feet 6 inches deep, and 2 feet 6 inches in diameter, was constructed of slabs set about the sides of a shallow excavation in the hard-pan. It contained the skeletons of an adult and an infant. The former lay on its right side, head south. The infant rested across the breast and left arm of the adult and had been wrapped in a fur-string blanket and placed in a skin bag. Both blanket and bag were in an advanced state of decay. There were traces of a woven bag that had once covered the remains of the adult. At one side of the cist near the head of the adult was a small bowl-basket containing beads and a variety of small objects, which are described elsewhere. There were also in the cist food offerings of corn and piñon nuts.

Cist 54. After removing from the surface a large number of rocks, the fill under the end of the great rock in the center of the cave was explored. Here, 2 feet below the under side of the rock in what appeared to be a rude cist, there was found a cradle in ex-cellent condition. With it were fragments of fur-string blankets and pieces of woven bags, but no trace of a body. The photo-graph, plate 5, a, shows the cradle *in situ*. The thin edge of the rock had been broken off somewhat before the picture was taken; it originally extended nearly a foot further than is shown. The rock may have broken from the roof centuries ago or in very recent times. The cradle, however, must have been in the position in which it was found when the fall occurred.

Summing up the evidence as to mortuary customs contained in the foregoing descriptions, we see that the bodies were placed in cists of three sorts: jar-shaped excavations, whose primary purpose seems to have been for storage; larger, shallower pits apparently dug expressly to contain burials; and slab cists of the type illustrated in plate 9, c. Almost every cist held more than one individual and all the indications pointed to the interments having been made simultaneously.[1]

The bodies of adults were always wrapped in fur-string blankets and at the loins of most females were small string aprons. The limbs were flexed to occupy the least possible space and occasionally held in that position by cords. The bundles thus prepared were encased in large woven bags, which were cut down one side for greater ease in drawing on, and then stitched together again with yucca leaves. Babies were sometimes placed in bags, but were more commonly buried on their cradles with their blankets, umbilical pads and "diapers" of bast in place as in life.

No fixed manner of orienting the remains was adhered to, this detail having been decided, apparently, by the manner in which the body best accommodated itself to the shape and size of the cist.

Mortuary offerings were numerous and varied and seem fairly representative of the food, implements, weapons and ornaments of daily life together with some objects of a ceremonial nature. The standard gift to the dead was basketry; tray baskets were practically always inverted over the heads of adults, often over children; large panniers also served as covers; and smaller baskets, empty or filled with trinkets, were generously piled into the graves.

Kiva (?). There remains to describe a peculiar and puzzling room found at the front of the cave (see figure 5). The first intimation of its existence came when, in clearing the surface above what proved later to be the ventilator shaft, the wall of the main structure was exposed. The room, as shown in the plan, lies at the foot of the great rock pile which rises at a sharp angle to the

[1] The same thing was noted in Sunflower Cave (Cists 7 and 11); in Cave 1 Kinboko (Kidder-Guernsey, 1919, p. 83) and in the Sayodneechee burial cave (Ibid. p. 29); at the latter site there were more individuals per grave than in any of the others, one cist holding no less than 19 bodies; all, apparently, buried at one time.

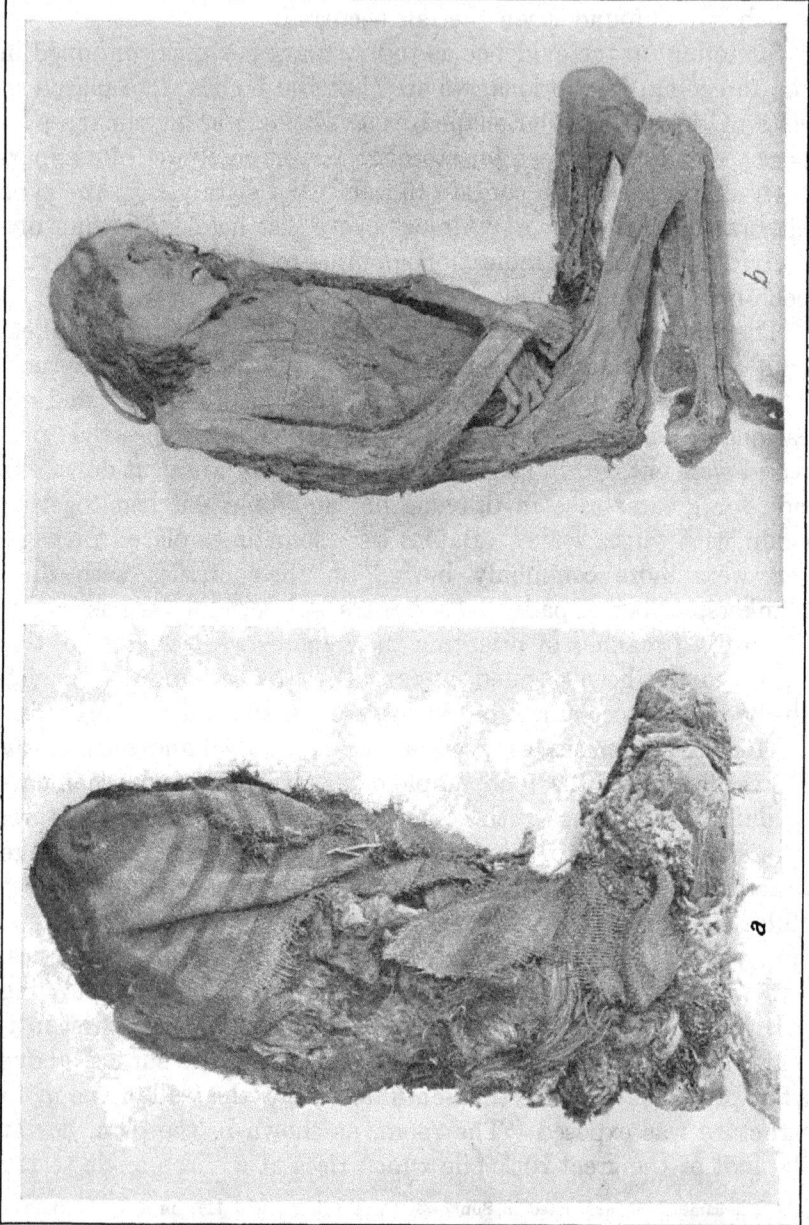

White Dog Cave

Mummy of man, Cist 24: a, Wrapped; b, With coverings removed.

back of the cave. It was owing to the imminent danger of rock slides from this source that we were unable to excavate the room completely, either in 1916 or on a second visit to the cave in 1917, when another attempt was made to do so.

This chamber is, and apparently always was, entirely subterranean. The part that we were able to clear is irregularly circular. The room is sunk through the surface sand and into the hard-pan, which, standing as dug, forms the lower part of the wall (see figure 7, b). The upper wall is masonry of rough and irregular

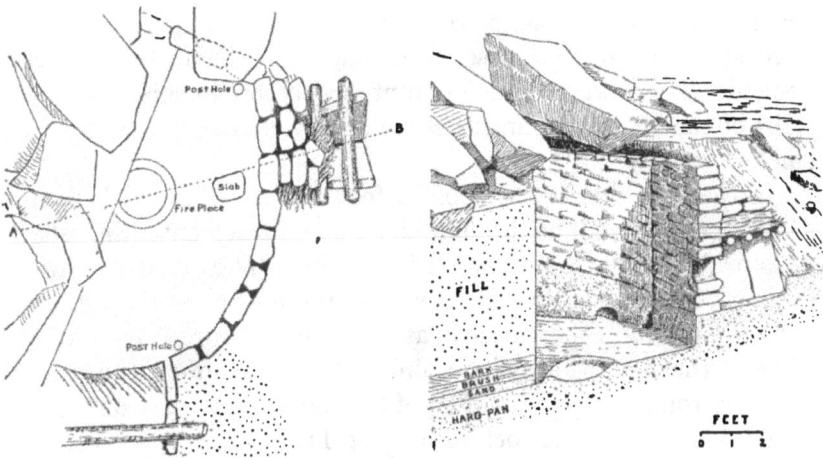

FIGURE 7
White Dog Cave: Plan and Cross-section of Kiva.

stones laid with little attempt to preserve a smooth face either within or without. At one point on the east side two upright slabs were set in and the wall was built on them. The top courses are somewhat more carefully constructed. Adobe mortar is used, sparingly below, more abundantly above. The whole structure is thickly "spalled" with small fragments of stone wedged into the cracks.

The general shape of the wall, partly straight, partly curved, can best be seen in the plan and section. The southern offset, which in the plan has the appearance of a bench or banquette, we are inclined to think was not a part of the original design of the builders, but was made necessary by the occurrence here of an outcropping of the ledge, the upper surface of which slanted inward at too

31

great an angle to furnish a stable foundation for a wall along the inner edge. At any rate, the offset overcame this difficulty, though for some reason, instead of continuing the wall as before, of laid-up stones, stone slabs set on end were used. We do not know whether or not this method of construction is continued under the rock pile. Placed across the top of the slabs was a stout log, one end resting on the top of the offset, the other passing out of sight under the rock heap. It is possible that the entrance to the room was at this point, as the sloping surface of the ledge here is very smooth as if from wear. South of the offset and outside the room we found slabs, set at right angles to the wall, and three upright stakes burned off close to the adobe in which they were embedded. There was a large amount of charcoal in this area. The slabs of the offset wall and those outside were much blackened by smoke.

On the east side of the room 2 feet above the floor, there is a small opening leading through the wall into a ventilating shaft. This orifice is five and one-half inches high by eight inches wide; it has two slender, round lintel sticks running across its top, their ends embedded in the masonry at either side (figure 7, b). All the edges of the opening are neatly finished off with adobe, the corners carefully rounded. On the floor of the room, nearly in front of this hole, lay a thin slab of rock measuring 11 by 12 inches; on trial it was found to fit exactly into grooves around the hole that had obviously been made for it (plate 10, b).

The horizontal shaft, to which the opening gave access, extended out from the wall for a distance of 3 feet 6 inches. It was built of flat stones set on either side with their bases together and their tops slanting outward, making a V-shaped trough 2 feet 6 inches wide across the top. This was roofed over with short stout logs covered with cedar bark, brush and coarse grass, the whole held down by flat rocks. The photograph, plate 11, b, shows the east end of the shaft with its log roofing. Behind and above may be seen the outside of the top courses of the wall of the main room, the position of which is also indicated by the dotted line in plate 11, a. There is no trace of a vertical flue connecting this horizontal passage with the surface. The pitch of the deposit is so steep here that it is probable that such a shaft was unnecessary, and that the horizontal passage ran straight through to the outer air.

32

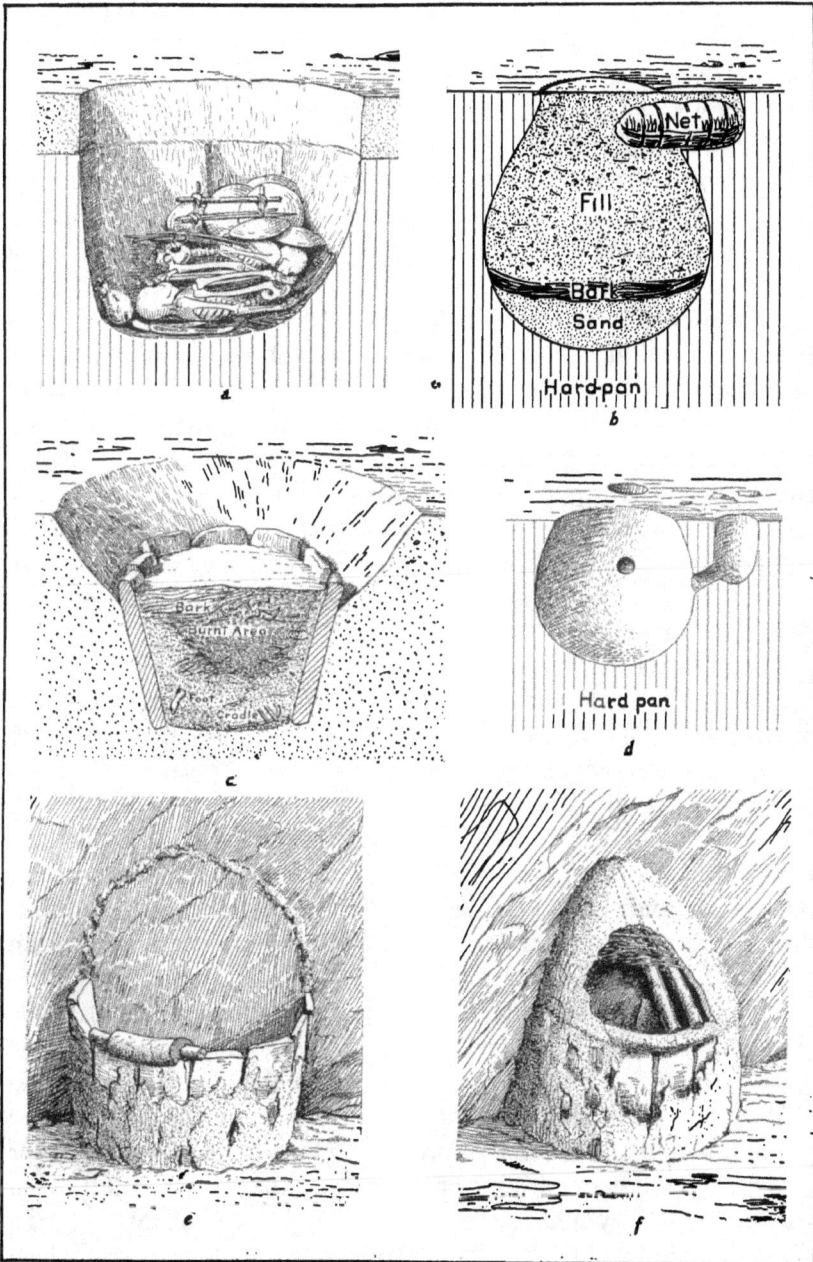

Types of Basket-maker cists: a, b, d, White Dog Cave; c, Cave 6; e, f, Cave 14.

The floor of the room itself, as far as we were able to lay it bare, was of hard packed adobe with a smooth but uneven surface. At what seems to have been a little east of the middle of the room there is a firepit, a saucer-shaped depression in the floor with a neatly made coping or rim of hard baked adobe (plate 10 a). It was filled to the brim with clean white ashes. In outline the pit is a perfect circle, 2 feet in diameter; the rim is raised 3 inches above the floor, and the bottom is somewhat scooped out giving a depth of 5 inches to the center of the pit.

At the floor level in the back of the room is an oval niche dug horizontally 12 inches into the hard-pan of the wall, and measuring 18 inches across the front (see figure 7, b). There are two holes five and one-half inches in diameter and twelve inches deep, dug in the floor, one at the angle of the back and east wall, the other at the front directly opposite. So close are these holes set to the wall that at the back the sides of the holes are continued up through the adobe of the wall for some 6 inches. For this reason we are quite sure they are intended for post-holes though no post ends were found in them.

The filling of the room was entirely free from rocks, showing that the great pile that now covers its rear portions and its northeast wall must have fallen after the place had already been deserted for a long time. On the floor was a 3-inch bed of pure sand; above this was an equal amount of coarse brush and charcoal, topped by a layer of cedar bark. The remaining 4 feet 6 inches to the surface was a homogeneous deposit composed of equal parts of rat dung and sand, laid down in perfectly regular, thread-like horizontal strata, separated from each other by thin layers of clean wind-blown sand.

The peculiar make-up of this fill has been a matter of much discussion between the authors. A plausible history of the fill might be that the room, with roof still intact, was abandoned for a period sufficient to allow the three-inch layer of clean sand to sift in and accumulate on the original floor, after which it was retenanted for a short time, the brush and bark brought in, and fires built, then vacated finally by man to become the rendezvous of rats through the long period which must have been required to build up the deep deposit of rat dung and sand found in it. During this latter period the roof remained; otherwise, instead of thin regular layers of apparently sifted sand, there would have been sand deposits of varying thickness, marking the occurrence of high winds such as we experienced while at work in the cave. Finally, and prior to the falling of the rocks from the ceiling of the cave, there came other visitors who found the roof a convenient source of fuel supply thus accounting for its complete disappearance.

Such a long discussion on the foregoing may appear unnecessary, but any condition which marks the lapse of time seems worthy of careful consideration.

It is unfortunate that we were unable to clear this room completely as there may be concealed beneath the débris which still covers the unexplored portion some evidence that would settle definitely the question of whether it is the work of the people who excavated the cists and buried their dead here, or of the Cliff-dwellers who came after. Such artifacts as were found in it are of little assistance in identifying the builders since they are either devoid of character or of such a nature as might easily have been dragged into it by rats. Outside the wall on the northeast and east sides we found some evidence of disturbance, such as might have been made in excavating for the foundation of the room, and in this disturbed area, close against the wall, lay two sandals with side-loops, of a type quite common in cliff-dwellings but which we have not yet found directly associated with Basket-maker remains. One of these was touching the wall at a depth of about 3 feet below the surface.

Had the chamber just described been found in a pueblo or cliff-dwelling, it would have occasioned no particular surprise, for while its ventilator opening is smaller and higher set than usual and the V-shaped horizontal passage is of unfamiliar construction, yet the mere presence of a ventilating apparatus, the adobe rimmed fireplace full of white ashes, and the subterranean situation of the room itself are all features perfectly normal in Cliff-dweller kivas. Furthermore the kivas of this particular district are typically variable and unspecialized.[1] The sandals seem to be Cliff-dweller and to have been left where found while the wall was under construction. All these things point to an origin subsequent to that of the Basket-maker cists. On the other hand we have never seen, nor have we read of, a kiva built as is this room all by itself

[1] Kidder-Guernsey, 1919, p. 201.

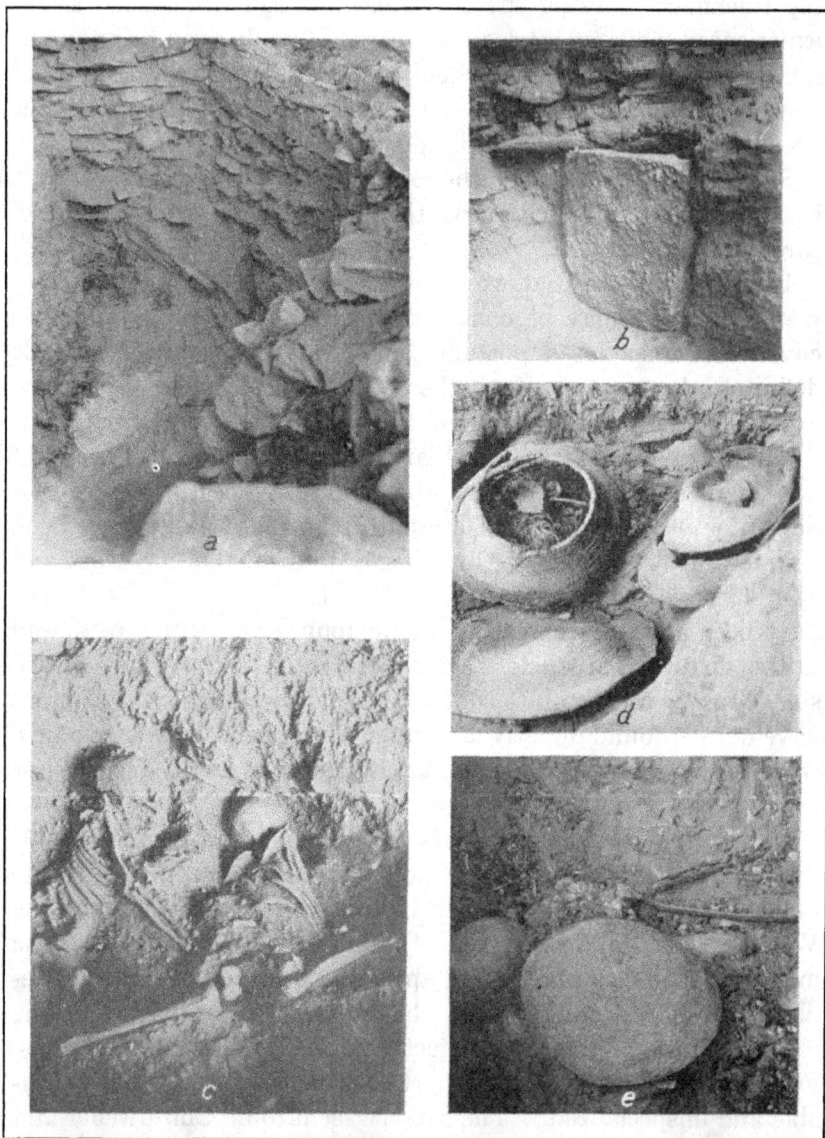

White Dog Cave: a, Interior of kiva; b, Ventilator cover in kiva; d, Baskets in Cist 22;
e, Objects in Cist 13.   Sunflower Cave: c, Skeletons in Cist 7.

with no living-chambers in the vicinity. All kivas with which we are familiar form integral parts of house-clusters. The only surely identifiable Cliff-dweller remains found in the cave are enumerated as follows:

A storage room foundation was built on the sloping rock floor against the west side of the cave (see figure 5); it measured 5 feet in length, 2 in width and consisted of a low wall, 8 to 10 inches high, the stones mudded in with adobe mortar. In the enclosure was a bed of plant stalks, "Brigham tea"; the floor is bare uneven rock. We collected in the top sand of the cave a few handfuls of Cliff-dweller potsherds, for the most part plain gray and black-and-white ware, and a few pieces of feather string. A small corrugated pot covered by a flat stone was found cached in the sand 1 foot 6 inches below the surface; the mouth had been sealed with adobe mudded on to corn cobs, but this had crumbled and was found at the bottom of the jar. About the jar was a harness, made, with the exception of one short section, of Cliff-dweller feather string. The short piece is apparently Basket-maker fur-string and was probably a stray bit picked up from the surface.

The above is not an imposing list and leads us to doubt that the place was ever regularly used as a dwelling by the Cliff-house people. As to the identity of the kiva-like room, the writers themselves are not agreed; the senior author believes that it may possibly be of Basket-maker origin, the junior considers it surely Cliff-dweller, but can offer no explanation for its isolated situation.

FIELD WORK, SEASON OF 1917

REACHING Kayenta by the usual route via Farmington, New Mexico, and the Chinlee, the party first attempted explorations near Sayodneechee Canyon in Monument Valley, but was forced by lack of water to abandon the work after a few caves had been examined. Returning to Kayenta the exploration of the South Comb was resumed. White Dog Cave was revisited and an unsuccessful attempt was made to move the rocks from above the kiva-like room. Two new caves were discovered and investigated. Again forced to move by lack of water, the remainder of the season was spent in Sagiotsosi Canyon, where nine caves were either wholly or partly explored (see map, figure 1).

SAYODNEECHEE CANYON

This is one of the numerous short canyons which head near the Agathla rock and run northward into Monument Valley. Although it is without living water, the Navajo are able to cultivate corn in certain places. In the winter, rain and melting snow furnish sufficient drinking water for the Indians and their flocks; and in some years enough of this is held in pockets among the rocks to last until the showers of July and August. Generally, however, these natural reservoirs go dry in June and the Navajo must move away for a month or so to some more favored locality, returning after the rains to harvest their crops.

Aside from its dryness, Sayodneechee is a most attractive place; the scenery is magnificent, grass and firewood are abundant, and the cliffs contain many caves to tempt the archaeologist's shovel.

Caves 3, 4 and 5 are in a break of the rock ridge that forms the west wall of Sayodneechee Canyon, and are nearly opposite the Basket-maker burial cave in the above canyon excavated by the 1914 expedition.[1]

Cave 3 is a mere shelter measuring 15 feet in depth by 30 feet in width. The wash of a small canyon has cut away the floor at the front. On the back wall are a number of pictographs done in white, red, and yellow paint; some of these are reproduced in plate 13, a. We found several slab cists buried beneath the sand floor. They contained nothing except cedar bark.

[1] Kidder-Guernsey, 1919, p. 27 and figure 1.

WHITE DOG CAVE
a, Rock pile in center of cave; b, Southern wall and ventilator in kiva.

Cave 4, a short distance up the canyon, is 20 feet above the wash. It has a depth of 12 feet and measures about 24 feet across the front. The floor is of hard-pan free from surface sand. In it are a number of small cists or pot-holes. At the front the hard-pan formation has a vertical break, in which is dug a small cubby hole measuring 4 feet in depth by 3 feet 6 inches in width. At the entrance to this little room, shown at the left in plate 12, a, are a number of flat slabs arranged like steps, a single slab 2 feet long and 8 inches wide serving for a sill. There are several small holes dug through the top of the room to the surface above. The largest of these holes is plugged with a rock.

A little further along the cliff is a rectangular Cliff-dweller room, the dimensions of which are, length 12 feet, width 7 feet, height of wall 6 feet 6 inches. In the center of the front wall is a doorway 29 inches high, 16 inches wide. At the top is a flat stone slab lintel supported by two round sticks built into the wall, another slab serves as a sill. The edges have grooves or jambs for the reception of a slab door. The masonry of this room is good. There were no pictographs. Potsherds were plentiful and along the cliff near the room there was some rubbish and a number of ash beds.

Cave 5 is still further up the canyon. It measures 45 feet across the front, and 15 feet in depth. At the back are the foundations of a room 10 feet long by 6 feet wide built out from the cliff. The masonry is of stones laid flat in adobe mortar. Two slab cists and two cists dug in the hard-pan floor were found in the cave, but no specimens.

Near the sites just described is a small shelter on the ground level of such insignificant size that no number was assigned to it in our field notes. We dug here, however, and at a depth of one foot below the surface found two slab cists partly filled with cedar bark. These were undoubtedly storage cists, as near by is a Navajo cornfield, located in a small basin which collects and retains such water as in time of rain runs off the surrounding cliffs, an advantage probably recognized by the early occupants of the region as readily as by the present day farmers.

The principal structures in these caves are of course Cliff-dweller. The slab cists and possibly some of those excavated in the hard-pan we are inclined to think are Basket-maker. No great amount of work was done at any of the sites, as we were on such short rations of water that our examination really only amounted to a reconnoissance. Continued drought finally drove us away, and we returned to the South Comb.

SOUTH COMB REVISITED

Cave 6. This site is in the next break in the Comb north of White Dog Cave, a distance of about one mile in an air line. It consists of a small alcove at the back of a huge crescent-shaped bay or cove in the cliff wall. Filling the open end of the crescent and hiding the cave from view in front is a high sand hill covered by a growth of thick brush and tall pines. The cliff on either side of the cave overhangs, sheltering a wide strip along the wall some fifteen feet lower than the floor level of the cave proper. On this level to the left of the entrance there is part of a roughly laid wall, built against the cliff. It forms a small enclosure and is probably the work of Navajo herders or possibly Ute, as on the smooth cave wall back of it are a number of drawings in charcoal (plate 13, f), one of which, a female figure, is shown wearing a dress that has characteristic features of the Ute woman's dress. Inside this enclosure were traces of recent fires and on the surface was a small mudded-up fire pit, which gave us the impression of having been the work of children.

The walls and ceiling of the inner cave are much blackened by smoke. It had been used as a sheep shelter and the old floor was covered by a thick layer of dung. The most careful search of the surface on the first level and the bank leading up to the cave proper failed to produce a single Cliff-dweller artifact and our excavations later showed not a vestige of Cliff-dweller occupation. Here for the first time we had a cave containing only Basket-maker remains, and while but a few specimens were found they were for the most part very true to type, the exceptions being entirely new material. A single burial was encountered. This was in a stone slab cist (plate 9, c), exactly like those found in such numbers in Cave 1, Kinboko (1915). Unfortunately, however, it had not only been plundered at some early date, but what remained of its contents had been partly destroyed by fire. The top of the cist was 18 inches below the surface. It measured 3 feet 4 inches in diameter at the top, 2 feet 6 inches in diameter at the

a, Structures in Cave 4 Sayodneechee Canyon; b, Cists in Cave 14, Sagiotsosi Canyon.

bottom, and was 2 feet, 4 inches deep. Ten slabs were used in its construction. In the upper part was a quantity of cedar bark and a few bones from the skeleton of a child, then a mass of charcoal and charred wood in which were fragments of human bones. On the bottom at one side was a partly burned cradle frame, and the mummified foot of an adult. Other objects found scattered in the fill are as follows: fragments of fur-string robe, dressed skin robe, twined-woven grass mat, string apron, a sandal, an atlatl, a grooved club, a skin-covered umbilical pad, the bark core of another, a skin bag, a bunch of human hair, a fragment of squash shell, and many small bits that could not be identified. All these specimens were more or less charred.

But one other slab cist was encountered. Its only unusual feature was a bottom lining of thin slabs of spruce bark.

Nearly all the level portion of the cave floor was occupied by a deep ash bed in which only a few minor specimens were found. Just outside this area at a depth of 1 foot 6 inches was a tray basket, and buried in the loose fill near it at about the same depth was the small woven bag in which was the little skin pouch shown with its contents in plate 44.

On the right of the cave the floor rises and narrows until it gives place to a mere bank of débris piled up against the back wall. At the highest point of this bank and next to the wall, three deer or possibly mountain-sheep snares were found. They had been cached in a shallow hole scooped out of the fill, and were covered with cedar bark and a thin layer of dirt. These snares are new items in our Basket-maker list. They are described and figured in another place (plate 32). A few feet from where the tray basket was found, and at the same depth, were three sherds of a substance resembling pottery of unbaked clay, tempered with shredded cedar bark, and bearing on one side the imprint of coiled basketry (plate 25, a). This may really be a primitive form of pottery or may represent only some left-over material for smearing joints in a slab cist, which was prepared outside the cave where both water and clay could be had, and then brought into the cave, while soft, in a convenient tray basket, from which it was not removed until it had hardened by drying. It is the nearest approach to pottery we have yet encountered under circumstances that would free it from suspicion of Cliff-dweller origin. Mr. John Wetherill, to whom it was shown, said it recalled the pottery found in the Basket-maker caves of Grand Gulch. This, according to McLloyd and Graham's description as quoted by Pepper,[1] was " a very

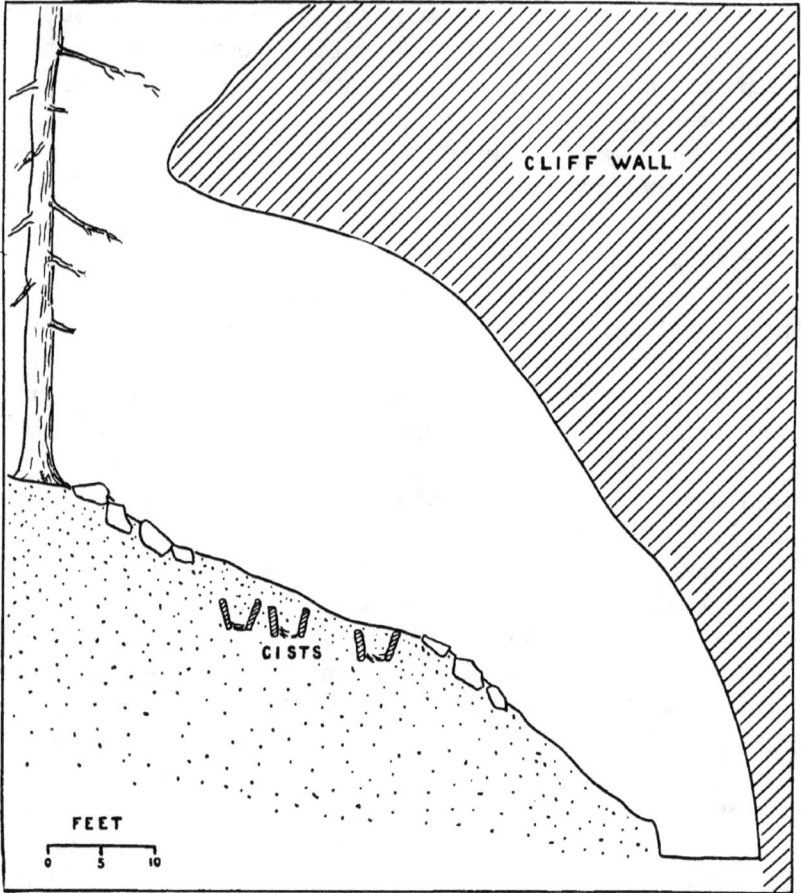

FIGURE 8

Cross-section of Cave 7, South Comb.

crude, unglazed ware, some of the bowls showing the imprint of the baskets in which they were formed."

As stated before, all our work in this cave brought to light not one trace of Cliff-dweller occupation, which includes not only potsherds, but also turkey droppings and turkey feathers, beans

[1] 1902, p. 9.

and rubbish layers. Hence the collection obtained here, though not extensive, is important as it supplies unmixed material with which to check our previous identifications.

Cave 7. About one mile north of Cave 6, we found another shelter very similar to it, except that it lacked the alcove room at the back. A steep hill rises directly in front of it. The slope of the hill next to the cliff lies almost wholly inside the line of shelter and its base at that point is cut away by an arroyo which continues along the wall for some distance. This seemed a very unpromising site, but on investigation we found a number of slab storage cists filled with cedar bark or grass, located as shown in the cross-section, figure 8. No Cliff-dweller remains were found here and only two Basket-maker specimens. These were the digging sticks shown in plate 37, e, f. This shelter seemed never to have been used as a place of abode for any great period as we found no extensive ash bed. Perhaps it was conveniently near some cornfield and was used only for storage purposes or as a temporary dwelling place while farming was in progress.

By the time that the work in Cave 7 was completed, the water in this section had become so bad that we were again forced to move.

SAGIOTSOSI CANYON

Sagiotsosi Canyon, though small in size compared with many others in this region, exceeds all that the writers have visited in the number of caves to be found in it and its branches. Its scenery is exceedingly picturesque, and it is rendered doubly attractive in this parched land by a stream of clear cold water fed by numerous springs that emerge from the base of the cliffs on either side at the upper end. This stream flows the entire length of the canyon finally to disappear in the thirsty sands just outside the entrance. In one place where it has cut a deep arroyo, a dark peat-like stratum can be seen in the vertical sides of the cut, marking an old lake bottom that probably once provided a natural reservoir for the ancient inhabitants. Today a number of well-irrigated Navajo cornfields and thrifty peach orchards show the water supply to be still ample for the requirements of primitive farming.

The caves in the main canyon are for the most part high up under the rim-rock and are perhaps more properly described as shelters. Some are of huge size with high arched openings, but of

45

no great depth. Occasionally they occur in groups of three or four, quite close together. To enter them one must first climb over huge fallen rocks to the first bench of the cliff, then up a steep talus of finer detritus to the caves, the bottoms or floors of which are really nothing but the truncated apex of the talus. Several of these caves have in them small Cliff-dweller structures. A number have already been explored by Professor Cummings.[1]

On the right about half way up the canyon and high in the cliff is a fair sized cliff-dwelling which to date has not been excavated. An interesting feature of this ruin is a tower that commands every approach to the cave. A cursory examination indicated that the roof had been destroyed by fire. On the back wall of the cave is a pictograph similar to the one illustrated in plate 13, e.

Cave 8. This cave is in the first branch-canyon leading out of Sagiotsosi to the west. It is in reality a shelter under the over-hang of the cliff, 30 feet in width, some 70 feet in length and about 25 feet above the bed of the wash. There is in it ample evidence of Cliff-dweller occupation, consisting of some foundation walls, a good depth of rubbish, with many potsherds, and a number of Cliff-dweller pictographs (plate 13, d, e); there is also a square-shouldered human figure done in white and yellow paint. This shows very faintly and a small Cliff-dweller painting of a snake overlaps it in one place (d). It was this square-shouldered picto-graph that induced us to dig here, as our previous experience had shown these figures to be of Basket-maker origin.

Our excavations disclosed considerable Cliff-dweller rubbish with hard-pan below it in which we found a number of cists, empty except for cedar bark or coarse grass. These cists and the square-shouldered figure are the only remaining evidences of Basket-maker occupation. From the general digging we obtained a num-ber of Cliff-dweller specimens including the skeleton of a young child on a perfectly preserved cradle which had been buried under the rocks at the top of the bank at the front.

This shelter seems insignificant in comparison to the huge caves in the main canyon. It provides, however, a further illustration of the fact that no cave or shelter in this region is so small that it has not at some time attracted tenants who have left traces of their occupancy.

[1] 1910, pp. 9–18.

Cave 9. Across the canyon from Cave 8 is a small Cliff-dweller ruin in a low cave that shows signs of previous investigation. Rooms along the back wall have been reroofed by the Navajo and used for storage purposes. This cave in the writers' opinion gives evidence of two occupations. This belief is, however, based wholly on the presence of typical Basket-maker cists excavated in the hard-pan floor (plate 14, c, d), for we found here no objects that could be classed as Basket-maker. The cists occurred in a small unoccupied area in the center and were completely filled with Cliff-dweller rubbish. There is, nevertheless, evidence at one place

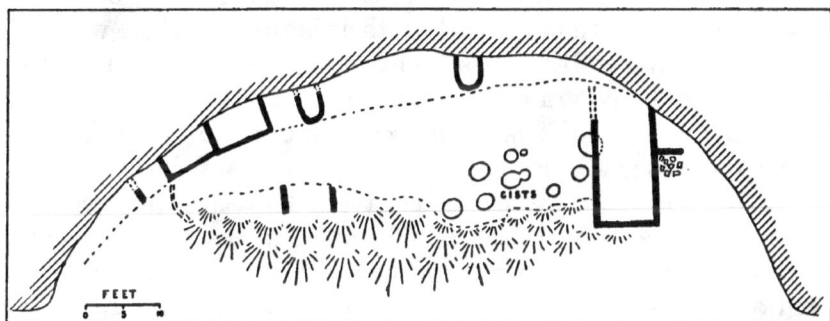

FIGURE 9
Plan of Cave 9, Sagiotsosi Canyon.

that the cists were here when the Cliff-dweller structures were erected, for the side wall of one room is built partly across a cist (see figure 9). The latter could hardly have been made by the Cliff-dwellers, since they could have easily avoided weakening the foundation of their wall by digging the cist a little to one side.

In objection to the foregoing it may be said that the cists are of Cliff-dweller origin; they are, however, exactly like ones found in other caves containing Basket-maker burials, and since all Basket-maker cists have a certain unity of design and a certain " look," hard to describe but at once apparent to anyone who has opened a number of them, the authors are satisfied that their identification of the present examples is correct. Compare c and d, plate 14 . with a and b of the same plate; the latter are from photographs of Basket-maker cists in White Dog Cave.

Cave 10. Just below Cave 8 there is a narrow break in the canyon wall with a length of perhaps 400 feet. About half way up this gulch is a shelter 20 feet in depth and 40 feet across the front (plate 5, b). The only sign of occupation noticed on entering was the top of a stone slab cist which just showed above the surface sand and a number of hand-prints in red on the back wall at one side. Excavation proved, however, that the place had been occupied by both the Basket-makers and the Cliff-dwellers. The Cliff-dweller remains consisted of a few potsherds, several bone scrapers of a typical Cliff-dweller form,[1] and a quantity of corncobs which we think are Cliff-dweller because they are much longer and larger than the Basket-maker corncobs we have found.

The Basket-maker remains were empty storage cists, both slab and excavated, with cedar bark in their bottoms. There was also one Basket-maker burial cist containing the partly mummified and headless body of a child, wrapped in a fur-string robe. With the body was part of a large dressed skin bag and at the feet lay badly rotted square-toed sandals. This burial was identical with those found in other Basket-maker caves. Evidence appeared that this or other cists had been plundered, as in the general digging there were found a number of fragments of Basket-maker basketry and a small piece of rabbit net made of human hair and fiber-string combined.

To gain entrance to the gully in which this cave is located one must cross a smooth, waterworn ledge. Up this is pecked a series of tracks representing the hoof-marks of a horse. They are very neatly executed and are the first instance that has come to our notice of pecked pictographs of recent (Navajo or Paiute) origin.

Cave 11. This cave is in the east wall of the main canyon near its head. It is some 200 feet above the wash and consists of a narrow shelter with a frontage of about 150 feet. On the back wall are a number of hand-prints and some nearly obliterated human figures all in white. On the surface were scattered a few bleached human bones. Large flat rocks along the front show deep axe-grinding grooves.

We were only able to spend a half day here. Our limited digging showed that for a considerable period the cave had been used by Cliff-dwellers and we recovered a number of their characteristic

[1] See Morris, 1919, figure 23, e. We found none of this variety in our cliff-house excavations in 1914.

Sayodneechee Canyon: a, Pictographs in white paint, Cave 3. Sagiotsosi Canyon: b, Pictograph in red paint, Cave 12; c, Pictographs in white paint, Cave 14; d, e, In white paint, Cave 8; f, In charcoal, Cave 6.

artifacts from the rubbish. At one point we found a loom-anchor in place. This consisted of a smooth pole one and one-half inches in diameter and six feet long, having loops of braided yucca and heavy fiber cord strung on it at regular intervals. It was buried several inches below the floor and held down by flat rocks, the tops of the loops just protruding above the surface. Under some large rocks at the front of the cave, we uncovered a small Basket-maker pannier basket in a poor state of preservation, inverted over a quantity of corncobs; probably the corn had been stripped by rodents. Attached to it was part of a carrying-strap of human hair string.

In a narrow part of the shelter and under what must have been the path ordinarily used in entering it, we found a disturbed Basket-maker burial. Some of the bones including the skull were missing. There were with the remains fragments of a coiled basket, square-toed sandals and a piece of finely woven cloth.

Cave 12. This is a deep cavern a short distance down the canyon from Cave 11 and on the same side. It is about 90 feet above the wash and has a fairly level floor area 40 feet deep by 70 feet across the front. The walls and ceiling are much blackened by smoke, and the floor is thick with charcoal. At one point the top of a rude enclosure of stone slabs shows just above the surface. This is circular in shape and has a diameter of 12 feet. At one place in the back wall are a group of hand-prints in red placed as near together as possible and covering a space of 6 feet or more; the only other pictograph noticed is the small figure shown in plate 13, b, also done in red. On a flat rock at the front are a number of axe-grinding grooves.

Our digging here was confined to test holes, as it was obvious that it would be too much of an undertaking for our small party to clear the cave completely. We found rubbish along the back wall to a depth of a little more than one foot. It was very compact and contained a large amount of broken sticks and twigs, straw and charcoal. There were two or three slab cists partly filled with cedar bark but holding no specimens.

We do not think any great returns would reward further work at this site. It had apparently been used by Basket-makers and Cliff-dwellers in turn, but did not appeal to the latter strongly enough to warrant the erection of any structures. It is set very deep in the cliff and gets but little sun; it may have been considered undesirable on this account.

Cave 13. This is a very long shallow shelter high up in the cliff near the head of the branch canyon in which Caves 8, 9 and 10 are located. At some not very remote time a great quantity of the roof had scaled off, burying almost the entire floor beneath tons and tons of rock. At one end of the cave is a series of small cliff-house rooms, some of which still retain roofs; others are crushed and the walls partly buried beneath the fallen rocks. Along the whole front of the cave can be traced a low roughly built wall. It seems probable that beneath the rocks are structures similar to those in the end of the cave, but to reach them would be a very large undertaking. We noticed no pictographs here.

Cave 14. This cave, the last to be explored, is but a short distance from Cave 13. It consists of a shallow shelter 200 feet above the canyon bottom, and has a usable floor space 20 feet deep by 70 feet in length. The line of shelter extends some 20 feet beyond the point where the floor breaks away at the front. At one end is a small niche in the back wall 7 or 8 feet above the floor. Leading up to it are a number of pecked toe-holes. The ceiling and some parts of the walls of the cave are blackened by smoke. On a smooth area of the wall near the center is a group of square-shouldered human figures painted in white, while other similar figures show faintly at other points (plate 13, c). These are distinctly Basket-maker. Built against the back wall of the cave is a series of seven stone slab structures, six of which are in a fair state of preservation. These will be given a more detailed description further on.

In our excavations here we found below the surface several slab cists of the usual Basket-maker type. From one we obtained a small skin pouch, which with its contents is shown in plate 38, a–c; also, in the loose fill, a wooden implement plate 36, a; and the bundle of human hair wrapped with string illustrated in plate 32, e. At the extreme right of the cave a single square-toed sandal was found in the general digging, and several ears of corn cached in the loose dirt against a large flat rock. So near is this cave to Cave 13 that it is inconceivable that it had not been frequented by Cliff-dwellers to some extent, yet careful search of the surface, and

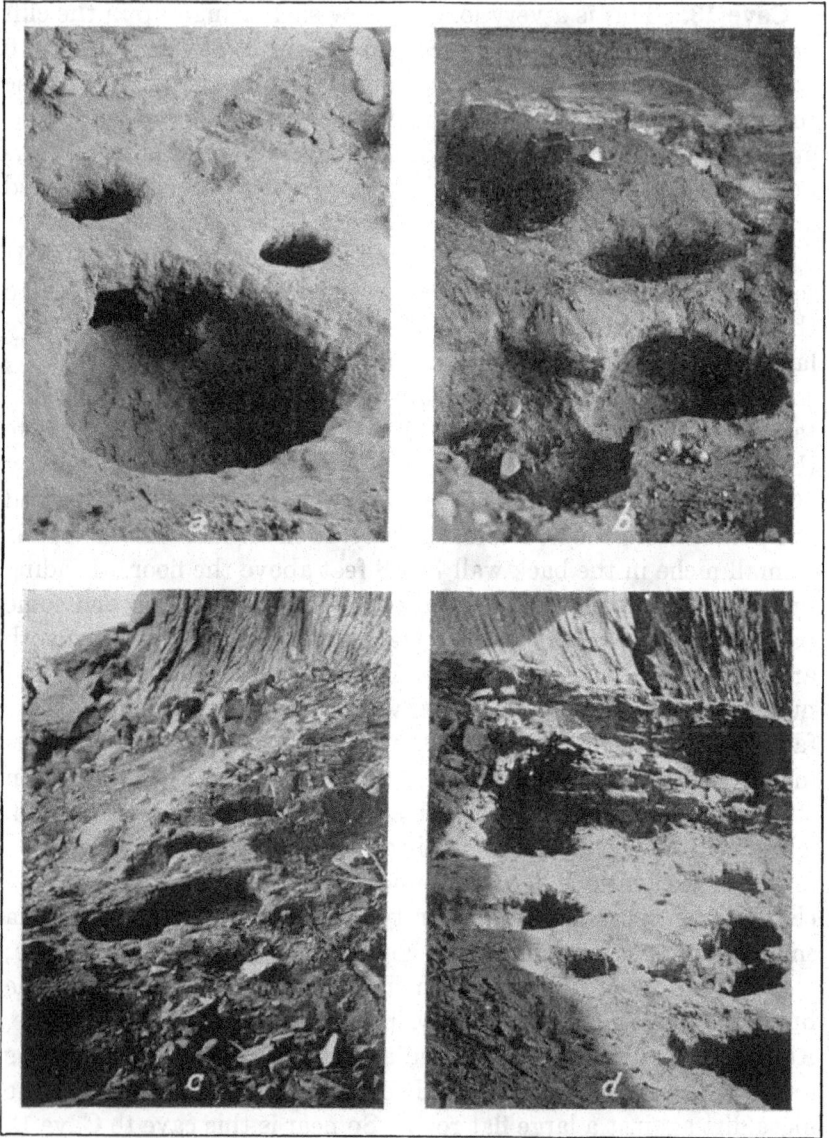

a, b, Cists dug in hard-pan, White Dog Cave; c, d, Cists, Cave 9.

watchfulness throughout the digging failed to produce a trace of their handiwork with the possible exception of the corn which may be Cliff-dweller, as it is unlike the characteristic Basket-maker corn. It was found in a part of the cave quite remote from the cists. There were no potsherds, twilled sandals, feather cloth or even axe-grinding grooves. The latter are seldom absent from caves in which the Cliff-dwellers have lived.

The most interesting things in the cave are the slab structures along the back wall (plate 12, b). They average about 5 feet in diameter, the best preserved standing three and one-half feet above the surface. Large stone slabs are used in their construction, in most cases overlapping. The space between the joints is filled with adobe mortar which in some instances has been plastered all over the slabs both outside and in. Small stones are set in to fill holes between the slabs and the cave wall to reinforce the slabs at their bases. In the structures and on the surface about them were a number of timbers from 4 feet 6 inches to 6 feet in length and 4 to 6 inches in diameter, probably roof timbers. Other shorter sticks were found which had once formed a part of a rim molded on to the top of the slabs. These pieces had traces of adobe on one side; there were also found large lumps of adobe tempered with cedar bark with one side moulded round, the other bearing imprints obviously made by the short timbers just mentioned. These sections of stick and adobe are important because they show that the present above-ground cists are identical in rim construction with a subterranean Basket-maker storage place (Cist 14) found in Cave 2, Kinboko during the 1915 season.[1] Another larger cist (12) in the same cave had a similar rounded adobe coping strengthened with stones instead of sticks. The drawing, plate 9, e, represents one of the Cave 14 cists with a short section of the rim restored. The slabs are shown partly denuded of the adobe plaster, while on the wall behind the cist a line of adobe is indicated which probably marks the outline of the roof. This structure more fully restored appears in f, of the same plate.

Why so much care should have been taken to finish the rim, if the roof timbers were to rest directly on it, we are unable to say, though it is evident that a rim made in this way would greatly

---

[1] Kidder-Guernsey, 1919, p. 88.

strengthen the whole structure. These slab cists seem hardly large enough for living rooms or even for sleeping places. It seems more probable that they were storage cists. We do not hesitate to identify them as Basket-maker, because they are exactly like the Basket-maker structures in Cave 2, Kinboko.

MATERIAL CULTURE [1]

FOOD

Vegetal Food. *Maize.* In 1914 and 1915 we found indications that the Basket-makers cultivated but a single and rather primitive type of corn, while that grown by the Cliff-dwellers seemed to have been more highly developed and more varied in character. Our evidence was not, however, absolutely conclusive, for certain specimens of the advanced corn were taken from Basket-maker caves, though from so near the surface that we regarded them as probably intrusive. The expeditions of 1916 and 1917 supply us, fortunately, with enough new finds to settle the question beyond any reasonable doubt. A number of Basket-maker caves were thoroughly investigated and many samples of corn were recovered from undisturbed and surely identifiable burials and storage cists; among all this material there is not a single kernel of any of the parti-colored flour or large white flint corns that are so common in the cliff-houses.[2]

On specimens submitted to him for examination Mr. G. W. Collins of the United States Bureau of Plant Industry has kindly given us the following report:

The collection of maize samples from the Basket-maker caves is of unusual interest.

The specimens all appear to belong to one general type, a type we have called Tropical Flint. This type resembles the New England flint varieties in having a large part of the endosperm hard or corneous. It differs from New England flint in having a larger number of rows and smaller seeds. Tropical flint varieties are common in Central and South America but are rare among the types grown by the Indians of the United States. So far as our collections show the Papago is the only tribe with varieties uniformly of this type.

The cobs of the specimens from the Basket-maker caves are all light brown in color. The pericarp is either red or colorless. The endosperm is either light yellow or white. The aleurone or layer of cells just beneath the pericarp in all the specimens is a yellowish red. This is a color entirely unknown in the aleurone of existing varieties. If this color is not the result of some slow disintegration, it constitutes the first clearly marked distinction between prehistoric maize and present day varieties.

Most of the specimens are remarkably well-preserved. The embryos have of course disintegrated but the colors are much brighter than is usual with old specimens.

---

[1] Only objects believed by us to be of Basket-maker origin are included. Specimens recovered from the cliff-houses will be treated in a later paper.

[2] See Kidder-Guernsey, 1919, p. 154.

The specimens cannot be referred to any existing variety with which I am familiar but with the possible exception of the unusual aleurone color they present no new characters.

Here then is an undifferentiated, and judging from its distribution, a primitive form of corn grown by a people whom the purely stratigraphic evidence shows to have antedated the highly developed agriculturists of the region. This agrees very well with the other manifestations of Basket-maker culture, and particularly with its lack of true pottery, stone architecture, and cotton weaving, all of which traits are characteristic of the perfected puebloan civilizations. We have thus good evidence that the Basket-makers were the pioneer corn growers of the district.

To what degree these people depended upon maize is uncertain, but quantities of it were found in the burial cists and cached for future use as food or for seed. There were also recovered agricultural implements such as would be needed for its cultivation, and the large number of storage cists in the caves would indicate by their capacity that a considerable harvest was obtained. The sites explored by us were all within easy reach of tillable land and this is also true of the Grand Gulch Basket-maker caves.

Of the actual finds of corn the best example is the skin bag full of shelled kernels from Cist 13, White Dog Cave (plate 15); there are about four quarts, every grain in perfect preservation. This may represent a food offering deposited with the dead, or perhaps it is carefully selected seed cached unknowingly in the same cist with the burials (it was found some 8 inches above the remains shown in plate 10, e). Other interments, however, were accompanied by corn and the remains of rotted hide containers, so that it may indeed be a food offering. A selection of the more perfect ears of Basket-maker corn is shown in plate 15.

Squash. This seems to have been the only other cultivated crop of the Basket-makers.[1] We unearthed with the burials varying quantities of squash seed, *Cucurbita pepo*, and many pieces of rind, as well as the complete vessel made from a squash shell that is shown on plate 31, b.

Seeds. In a number of the burial cists in White Dog Cave, large quantities of coarse grass seed were found. We saw growing in the

---

[1] Though we were constantly on the watch for beans in the Basket-maker sites, none were found. This strengthens our belief that they were not grown by the Basket-makers.

vicinity, the same variety of grass from which it was obtained. Mr. W. E. Safford of the Bureau of Plant Industry identifies this as follows:

> Oryzopsis hymenioides, commonly called Indian Mountain Rice, is used by several Indian tribes for food; by some only in times of scarcity, by others as a regular food staple. Mr. F. V. Coville states that the squaws of the Panamint Indians of southern California gather it by means of a wicker paddle resembling a small tennis racket with which they beat the seeds from the standing grass into wicker baskets, after which they are winnowed and sifted, and parched and ground into *pinolli*. The late Dr. Edward Palmer found this seed in use among the Paiute and Pueblo Indians, who store it for winter use.

Cummings[1] found caches of seed in Sagiotsosi ("coarse bunch grass"), which may be the same. No doubt other seeds were gathered and stored for food, as we found in 1915 several quarts of *Coreocarpus* seeds in a burial cist in Cave 1. Powell in his explorations of the Colorado found a tribe which subsisted chiefly on wild fruits, nuts and native grains. In our own explorations we came upon an old Navajo squaw in the vicinity of Sagiotsosi who was gathering the small seeds of a low weed. She told us that these were cooked and made into a kind of mush by mixing with goat's milk, also that they were now (1917) being used again for the first time since the "great war" (Navajo war, 1863). These are identified by Mr. Safford as *Chinopodium sp.*, who writes as follows regarding them:

> They are perhaps the most interesting of the collection. It has been impossible to determine their specific identity. They are much larger than the seeds of *Chenopodium fremontii*, gathered for food by the Klamath Indians, and those of *Chenopodium leptophyllum* eaten by the Zuñi. In shape they bear a close resemblance to the seeds of *Chenopodium quenua*, the well-known food staple of the Peruvian and Bolivian Plateau, but they are of smaller size and of a much darker color than the latter. These seeds have been carefully compared with those of the species growing commonly in the southwestern United States; they bear a closer resemblance to *Chenopodium petiolare* than to any other species in the herbarium, but they do not seem to be identical with the seeds of that species. They are evidently rich in starch and would undoubtedly form a nutritious article of food.

Piñon Nuts. These were also an important item of diet and were found with other food offerings in many of the graves.

---

[1] Cummings, 1910, p. 14.

Unidentified Food. Small quantities of plant stalks, shriveled beyond recognition, accompanied some burials. These are probably from certain edible plants that grow in the region, and which are eaten today by the Navajo.

Animal Food. The bones of mammals and birds, generally so common about the dwelling places of primitive people, were entirely lacking in the group of Basket-maker caves examined. We do not believe that this indicates a preponderatingly vegetarian diet, but rather that it proves the caves to have been used merely as temporary shelters and as burial places for the dead. That these people killed a great deal of large game is evidenced by the abundance of articles made from the hides of deer and mountain-sheep; while quantities of the pelts of badgers, rabbits, prairie-dogs, and other small animals were employed for bags, pouches, and in fur-string robes. It is probable that the flesh of all the above was eaten.

As to the birds we have less evidence. Such feathers as were found came principally from hawks and owls, species not commonly relished as food by any people; or from very small birds of bright plumage such as warblers, bluebirds, and woodpeckers. As we have never come across a single identifiable turkey feather, it is reasonably certain that the turkey was not domesticated, nor indeed does it appear to have been commonly hunted.

Although there is no evidence that the Basket-makers used the dog for food, it may be well to refer here to the finding of two remarkably well-preserved dog mummies in White Dog Cave. They represent different types, formerly of wide distribution in the warmer parts of America (plate 15). Dr. Glover M. Allen of the Museum of Comparative Zoölogy, who has made an exhaustive study of the native Indian dog, has kindly contributed the following regarding these specimens:

The larger is a long-haired animal the size of a small collie, with erect ears and long bushy tail. The hair is still in good condition and though now a light golden color, with cloudings of dark brown, it may in life have been darker. It is, apparently, a breed very similar to the long-haired Inca dog found at Ancon, Peru, in a mummified condition and described by Nebring (*Sitzb. Ges. Naturf. Freunde*, Berlin, 1887, pages 139–141). The latter specimen is also described as yellowish in color, though this may have been in part due to fading. A more detailed comparison of the two specimens is not possible without removing and cleaning the bones and so injuring the present example for exhibition purposes.

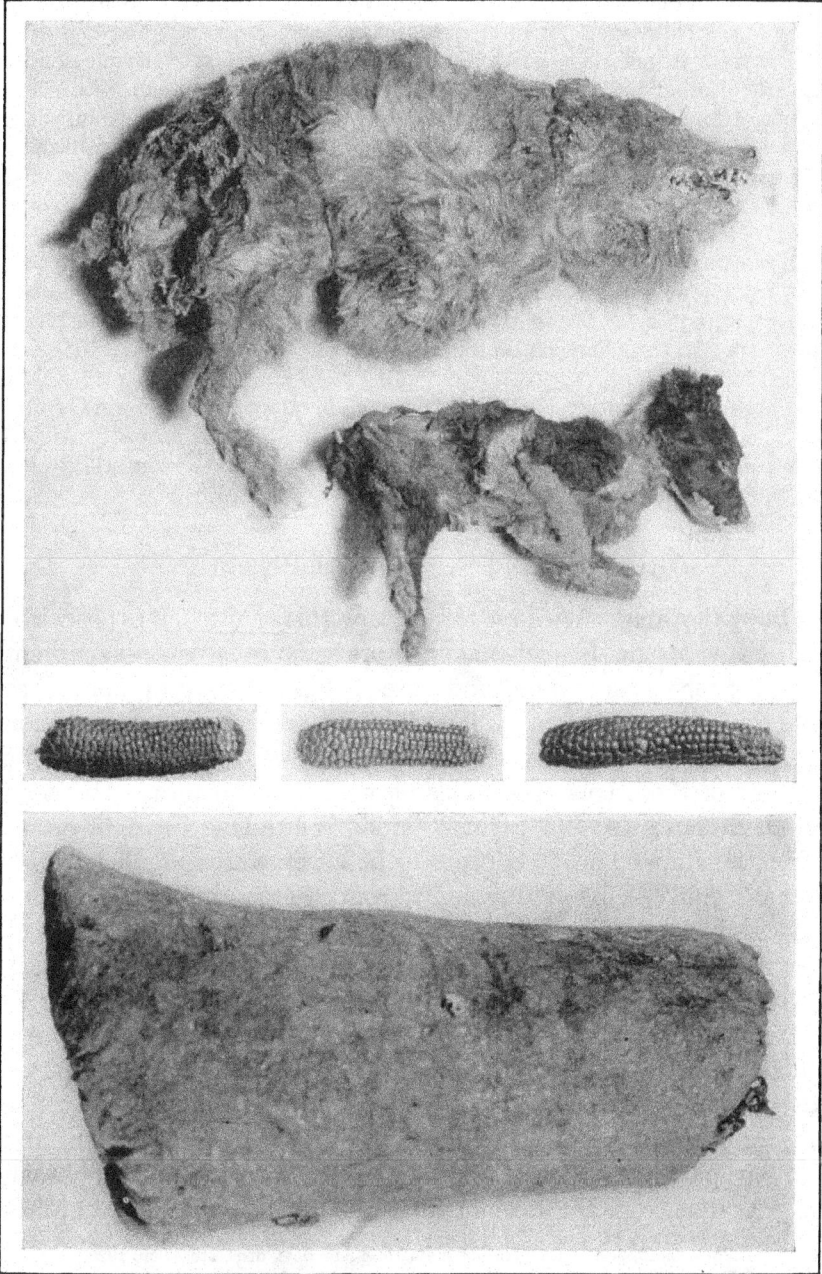

WHITE DOG CAVE
Mummies of two varieties of dogs, ears of corn, and skin bag containing shelled corn.

The other dog is a much smaller, black-and-white individual, about the size of a terrier, with short, but not close, shaggy coat, erect ears, and long full-haired tail. Its muzzle is rather short and stubby in contrast to the fine slender muzzle of other Indian dogs of about the same size. In common with many skulls of American Indian dogs, the first premolar is lacking in the adult dentition of the lower jaw. This specimen is of especial interest as establishing beyond doubt the identity of certain dog bones from Ely Cave, Virginia, described as *Pachycyon robustus,* for they agree perfectly with corresponding parts of the Arizona dog. An identical breed is represented among the mummified remains of dogs from the necropolis of Ancon, Peru, and has been figured by Nebring as *Canis ingae vertagus* in the folio report of Reiss and Steubel, plate 118, figure 1. Evidently it had a wide distribution in our south and southwest, and was known also to the Peruvians. I have called this the short nosed Indian Dog.

These and other dog remains, are true dogs, in no way derived from Coyotes or other native dog-like animals of America. Their forebears probably reached America with their human masters, but their Old World ancestors still remain to be determined.[1]

DRESS AND PERSONAL ORNAMENTS

Body Clothing. We have few data on this subject; it is probable, indeed, that the Basket-makers wore very little clothing except robes of fur-string or hide,[2] and "gee strings" or cord aprons. It so happens that all the robes found in sufficiently good preservation to permit of measurement had been interred with babies; the largest of these (plate 16, a) is only 25 by 23 inches. About an adult mummy (A–2939) from Cist 22, White Dog Cave, however, there is wrapped what appears to be a very large blanket of fur-string; and we have fragments from deer and mountain-sheep hides which seem to have been originally of ample size for use as mantles by grown people.

Nothing resembling fitted garments of leather or cloth has so far come to light; it is possible, however, that certain woven fabrics, bits of which were recovered from the caves [3] may have been used as ponchos. This guess is based on the resemblance between a zigzag decoration on one of the cloth specimens (plate 26, c) and similar patterns painted on the chests of Basket-maker human pictographs from the Monument country.[4] It must be admitted,

---

[1] For a discussion of the types of prehistoric American dogs, see Allen, 1920.
[2] For details of the weave of these robes, see p. 65.
[3] See plate 26, b, c.
[4] Kidder-Guernsey, 1919, figures 100, 101.

however, that the zigzag was a favorite Basket-maker design, and that the marks on the pictographs may perfectly well represent body-painting.

A string apron recovered by the 1915 expedition still remains our best specimen of this type. Although it was illustrated in our former report (plate 66, a), we have since succeeded in unraveling it for a somewhat clearer photograph; this, with a picture of a second example from the general digging in White Dog Cave, are here reproduced (plate 16, c, d). It will be seen that in both cases there is a waist cord to which is attached a fringe of pendent strings. In the 1915 specimen the strings are of apocynum and are looped over the human hair waist cord and gathered in bunches of about three hundred; the fringe is 12 inches long.[1] The apron from White Dog Cave (plate 16, c) is more fragmentary; the yucca-fiber waist cord is double; over it are hung yucca strings which are gathered together in pairs and held, close under the waist cord, by a row of twined weaving, one strand yucca, the other human hair. Although somewhat longer than the first apron this garment is much thinner and contains fewer strings.

Plate 16, b, shows part of a similar skirt made of cedar bark. The pendent strands are about 12 inches long and are held together by a twining of twisted cedar-bark string, the prolongations of which once formed the waist cord.

As the term apron implies, the fringes of these articles did not extend all the way around the body, but merely covered the front of the waist; it is probable that they hung loose, for the strings are too short to have been pulled between the legs and fastened over the waist cord behind. They are evidently a woman's garment, as in every case where they were discovered in place on a mummy, the body proved to be that of a female. Though we have never found any covering at the loins of a male, there are in the collection two objects that may well have been the ties of "gee strings." One is a loose twist of thirty animal wool threads (plate 16, f); it is nearly 7 feet long and its ends are tapered as if for knotting. The other is 5 feet 2 inches long and made of fifty to sixty thin strings of human hair; the ends are seized with fiber thread to prevent raveling.

[1] For a fuller description, see Kidder-Guernsey, 1919, p. 157.

Clothing: a, Fur cloth blanket; b, Apron of shredded bark; c, d, Aprons of fiber string; e, f, String belts. All from White Dog Cave except d, f, which are from Kinboko Canyon, Marsh Pass. (About ⅛.)

Sandals. As most of the specimens recovered by the 1916 and 1917 expeditions are very badly rotted and as no new types appear, the reader is referred to the classification and descriptions of the 1914, 1915 material given in the previous report.[1]

Necklaces. These were of two sorts: strings of beads; and twisted skin or fiber cords, to the middle of which were attached a few pendants or extra handsome beads. Of the latter class there was recovered only one fragmentary example (plate 17, b); it bears two very beautifully polished lignite discs strung on a fiber cord, which is itself attached to a sinew-bound thong; the whole was probably fastened to a longer neck cord as was done with a similar specimen found in 1915.[2]

The second type is more fully represented, several strings of beads having been taken from the necks of skeletons in White Dog Cave. A selection is given in plate 25, e–h. The most interesting of these is composed of seventy-one thick discoidal black lignite and white limestone beads strung alternately on a narrow thong. They are graduated in size from a maximum diameter of $\frac{5}{8}$ of an inch at the center of the string, to $\frac{3}{8}$ of an inch at the ends. An unusual refinement of technic was practised by cutting several of the beads to a wedge-shape (see figure 10, c, and plate 25, h) and introducing them here and there throughout the set in order that it might hang evenly. Loose behind the neck of the mummy who wore this string were fourteen olivella shells that apparently had once been fastened together to form a sort of " dangler " attached to the tie-strings of the necklace.

Another string (plate 25, f), which was recovered in order, is made of one hundred little saucer-shaped shell beads (figure 10, g); seventy-five thin, roughly discoidal shell beads (figure 10, f); and eighteen olivella shells, one of which bears an incised zigzag decoration (figure 10, i). These different kinds of beads were grouped together. Plate 25, e, shows a third necklace composed of ninety-five beads arranged as follows: one of lignite, seven olivella shells, one of seed, one of bone, one of red shale, one of green shale, one of red shale, eighty-one of white limestone. Plain strings of olivellas designed to go once or twice around the neck are not uncommon.

[1] Kidder-Guernsey, 1919, pp. 157–160.

[2] Kidder-Guernsey, 1919, p. 161 and figure 72, a. A full description of this type of necklace is there given.

Beads. Under this head are considered all the beads found, whether strung into necklaces, discovered loose in the cists, or included in "medicine outfits." The commonest of all are little cylinders averaging $\frac{3}{16}$ of an inch long (figure 10, e, and plate 25, g); some are of albatite, a phase of asphaltic shale, but the great majority (hardly distinguishable from the above except under a magnifying glass) are made from some hard black seed so cut down in manufacture as to be unidentifiable. Other seeds were used un-

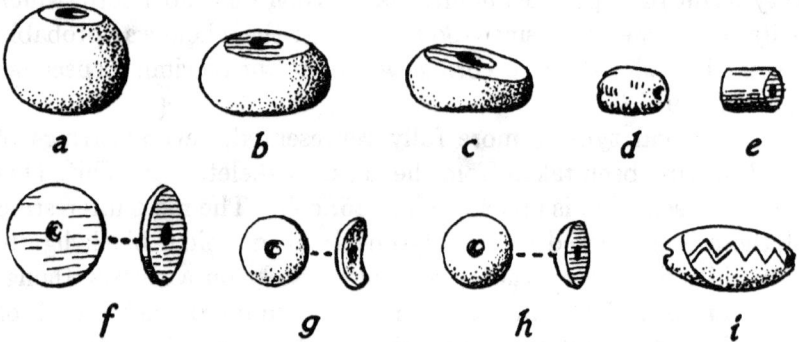

FIGURE 10
Beads from White Dog Cave. (Full size.)

worked except for a narrow bore.[1] Two varieties of these seed beads are identified by Mr. Safford:

> The first is the polished white nutlet of *Onosmodium occidentale*, a plant of the Borage family, belonging to a genus not far removed from *Lithospermum*. These beautiful little nutlets may well be called pearl-seeds, since when strung they must bear a close resemblance to small seed-pearls. Accompanying these is a small longitudinally grooved dull brown seed, somewhat resembling the seeds of the bead tree (*Melia azederach*) in form. The terminal scar is removed by the perforation, and it has been impossible to identify this, or even to determine to what botanical family it belongs.

Stone beads are of fine-grained white limestone, lignite, serpentine, quartz, hematite and alabaster. Most of them are large, no minute beads, such as those from Aztec[2] or the Upper Gila,[3] occurring. In shape they run from the flattened spherical type (figure 10, a)[4] to the more or less thickened discoidal form (figure 10, c).

[1] See also Kidder-Guernsey, 1919, plate 70, k, a string of acorn cups.
[2] Morris, 1919, p. 99.   [3] Hough, 1914, p. 24.
[4] Wrongly called "hemispherical" in our former report (p. 163).

Most of the shell beads were made from olivellas simply by cutting off the end of the spire. There are in one of the strings (plate 25, f) seventy-five very thin disc-shaped beads, $\frac{7}{16}$ of an inch in diameter cut, apparently, from the shell of a fresh-water clam (figure 10, f). The same necklace contains one hundred shell beads made from the curving wall of the large olivella (figure 10, g). The saucer-like form of these allows them to fit closely over each other when strung. Enormous quantities of identical beads are in the Museum's collection from the Channel Islands, California. There are a few small bone beads (figure 10, h) apparently made in imitation of these.

Pendants. These were less common in the burial cists of White Dog Cave than they were in the mortuary cave of Sayodneechee.[1] The single stone specimen (plate 17, h) is of a hard brown stone mottled with brownish green; the surface is highly polished and has a waxy texture.

Four shell pendants were found, all of abalone; three are illustrated in plate 17, c, d, e; the fourth is attached to a ceremonial object (plate 39, b). The largest (plate 17, c) is round and 2 inches in diameter. It has two perforations in the center from which radiate the four arms of an incised cross figure. Along the edge are two other round holes and three pairs of minute perforations. At the bottom of this disc there is a drilled hole which has been stopped up by inlaying a little piece of abalone shell carefully shaped to fit the aperture. The second abalone pendant (plate 17, d) is the reused half of a disc similar to the above; it fractured, apparently, along an incised median line. Traces of the favorite Basket-maker zigzag may be seen along the upper edge of the old break. The third specimen (plate 17, e) is a bit of the thickened rim of an abalone, the edges ground down and polished.

Feathered Pendant. This object (plate 18, f) is described under the head of personal ornaments although it may have served some other, possibly ceremonial, function. It consists of nine two-ply twists of rawhide thong, seized with sinew to a loop of the same material. Small feathers, whose butts alone remain, were once fastened to the ends of the streamers.[2]

---

[1] See Kidder-Guernsey, 1919, p. 164.
[2] Compare Kidder-Guernsey, 1919, figure 77.

Ornament of Mountain-sheep Horn. This object (plate 17, i) is 3 inches long by 2½ wide. The convex side shown in the drawing bears, besides two pairs of drilled perforations, a double series of small holes which do not run through. Incised lines drawn between the two series, seem to show a start at a zigzag decoration. The toothed ends of the specimen were produced by sawing broad notches along the upper and lower edges. The bottoms of the notches are well worn and smooth, but whether from general use or from friction of threads (supposing the object to have served as a weaving comb), we do not know.

Deer-hoof Rattles. As in the preceding two cases, the identification of these specimens (plate 17, j, k) as ornaments is open to question; a ceremonial use is quite as likely. One of them consists of the horny outer coverings of two large hoofs, attached to the ends of a buckskin thong.[1] The other shown in j is made of much smaller hoofs; these are fastened to the ends of thongs which themselves are looped over a slim pliable twig and held to it by a twining of fine cords. This is an incomplete specimen, as is another similar one (not figured, A–2930) which had, in place or detached, nearly a hundred hoofs. There is little doubt that the stringing together of these dry resonant hoofs was done to produce a rattling sound, but whether the assemblages were employed as belts, as fringes, or fastened to handles to form true rattles we have no means of telling.

Unfinished Ornament. This object (plate 35, h, i), found in the general digging in White Dog Cave, is a neat example of two processes in working stone: flaking and grinding. The specimen is a disc of grey flint, convex on both sides. It was first chipped roughly to its present form, then ground to efface the chipped surface. The grinding process was, however, not completed and there remain on either side marks of chipping, as well as numerous grinding facets.

Tablet. Plate 17, a, shows, partly restored, a tablet-like object of compact white limestone found in Cist 6, White Dog Cave. The pieces fitted together have a length of 7 inches, but a number of fragments that could not be joined show that the original length was considerably more; the greatest width is 3 inches, the thickness

[1] Modern Hopi hoof rattles are figured by Hough (1919, plate 22).

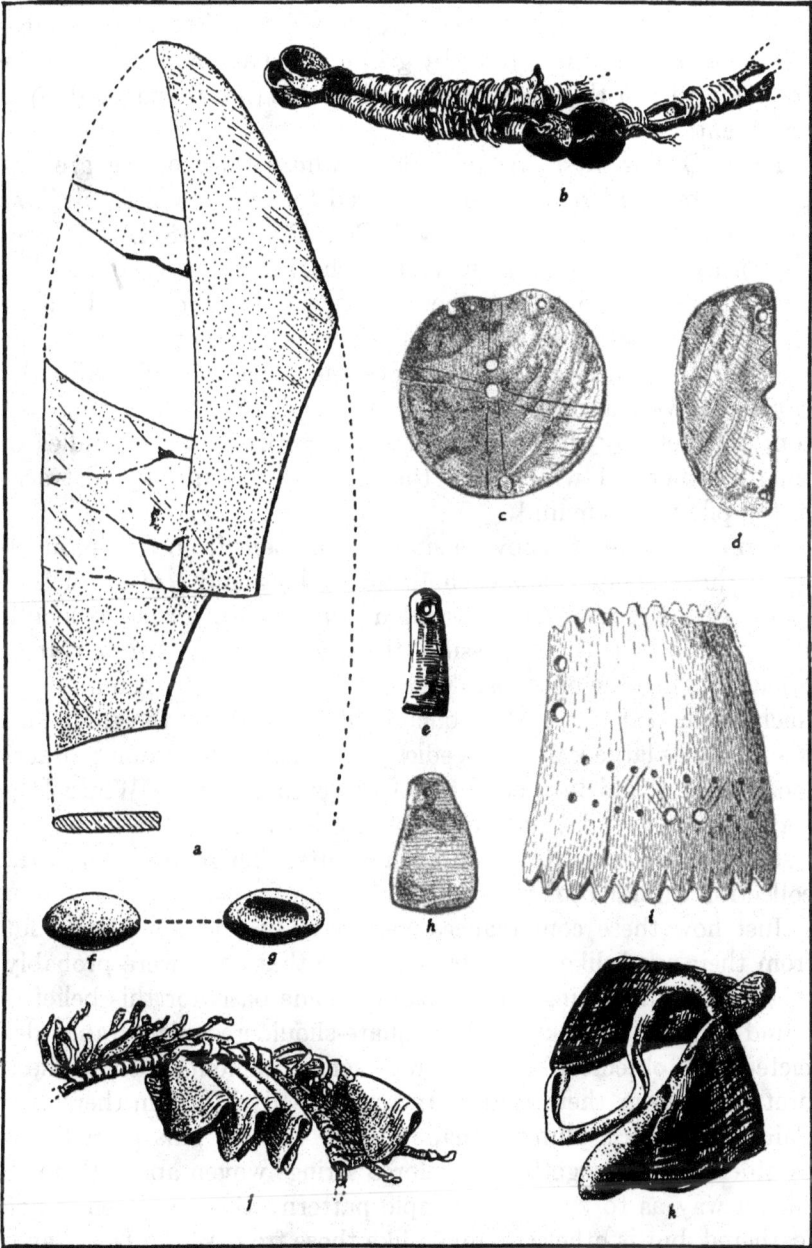

WHITE DOG CAVE

a, Tablet-like object of stone; b, Neck ornament; c, d, e, Shell pendants; f, g, Object of stone; h, Stone pendant; i, Object of mountain-sheep horn; j, k, Hoof rattles.   (About ½.)

uniformly $\frac{3}{16}$ of an inch. The edges are rounded and all surfaces very smoothly worked down by grinding. The fine finish and the fragile nature of this object seem to indicate that it was used as an ornament.

Head Ornaments. An object, of whose function we are not positive, but which was probably used to decorate the hair, was found on the breast of mummy 2, Cist 27 (plate 18, b). It consists of five neatly made bone pins, each $5\frac{1}{2}$ inches long and a little less than $\frac{1}{8}$ of an inch in diameter, fastened together side by side. The bindings are of sinew; the upper set is overwrapped with fine fiber cord evidently as a finish, since the string, though badly decayed, shows traces of a central red band. Projecting from the top, and held by the wrappings just described, were bundles of small feathers, of which only the butts of the quills and traces of the pile now remain.[1]

Figure a, plate 18, shows a similar ornament from Cist 6, made up of three wooden pins each 10 inches long and $\frac{1}{8}$ of an inch in diameter. A bundle of six wooden pins, each 8 inches in length and $\frac{1}{8}$ of an inch thick, possibly ready to be made into a pair of ornaments like the ones just described, is figured in c. A number of finely fashioned but broken bone objects, of about the same size and shape as large knitting needles, some tied up in bundles, others loose, were found in the course of the excavations in White Dog Cave; most of them show signs of long use. These no doubt are also unassembled parts of head ornaments. There are in the 1915 collection similar broken bone pins.[2]

Just how these contrivances were worn we do not know, but from their comb-like structure we judge that they were probably stuck in the hair, singly or in pairs. Some basis for this belief is found in certain Basket-maker square-shouldered pictographs depicted with objects which may represent ornaments such as these protruding from their heads.[3] In the Peabody Museum there is a Paiute "warrior's plume," made of five wooden pins placed side by side and held together by colored strings woven about them in such a way as to produce a simple pattern; this specimen is not feathered, but is otherwise much like those from White Dog Cave.

---

[1] A fairly well-preserved example from Grand Gulch is in the American Museum of Natural History, New York (cat. no. H–13375).
[2] Kidder-Guernsey, 1919, plate 86, e.
[3] Ibid., figure 101.

BASKET–MAKER CAVES

In the Coahuila, Mexico, cave collection in the Museum there is an arrangement of six wooden pins which may be either a head ornament or a comb; we are inclined to think the former, as the same collection contains an object that is surely a comb, constructed in an entirely different manner.

The object shown on plate 18, d, may be an ornament, a projectile for a dart game, or possibly a ceremonial object; it is a thin twig with three small feathers seized to it at their butts and tips by sinew; the ends of the stick are broken off, so that its original length is unknown.

Hair-dressing. Several of the mummies from White Dog Cave are in so good a state of preservation that their heads still retain the hair, dressed, probably, as in life. On plate 19 are illustrated the various methods; figures a, b, c are drawn from mummies, and d, is restored from a scalp found in the same district in 1915.[1]

Figure a, shows the simplest manner of wearing the hair, which in this case is cropped to an average length of 2 inches. The raggedness of this haircut is apparently the result of gathering together and hacking off a single lock at a time. The individual in question was a female about twenty years of age found in Cist 22 (mummy 2).

Figure b, shows the arrangement of the hair of an adult male from Cist 24. It is parted in the center from forehead to crown and falls loose on either side; that of the back of the head is gathered into a queue, the end of which is turned back on itself and wrapped for a space of 2 inches with a fine string. From the crown there hangs a lock the thickness of a pencil closely wound with string for nearly its entire length.[2] The end of this tress is bound up with the end of the queue. Where this lock grows from the scalp, the surrounding hair is clipped away for a little space.

Figure c, is drawn from the head of a male about twenty-five years old, from Cist 22. The hair is arranged as follows: from a strip 1½ inches wide straight back from the middle of the forehead the hair has been cut off close to the scalp. This exaggerated " part " terminates at the crown in a circular tonsure in the center of which there is a thin lock of long hair. The hair on either side

[1] For pictures of this interesting specimen, and for a description of its preparation, see Kidder-Guernsey, 1919, plates 87, 88, and pp. 190–192.

[2] As was noted on p. 13, a section of a similar lock wound spirally with a leather cord was found in Cist 6, White Dog Cave.

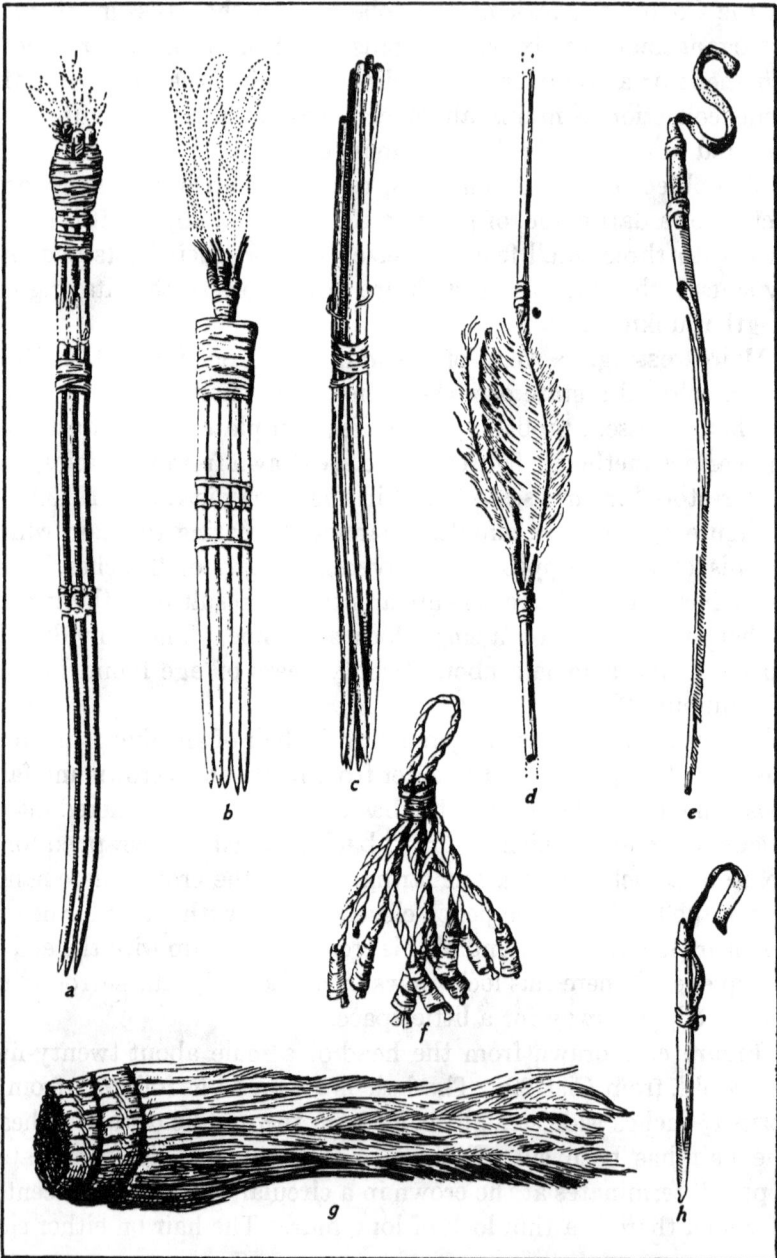

WHITE DOG CAVE

a, b, d–g, Feather ornaments; c, Package of wooden pins, probably used in making
feather ornaments.   (About ⅓.)

of the " part " is gathered together and tightly bound 3½ inches from the ends with fine human hair string; these tresses hang in front of the ears. The back hair, which is about 14 inches long, is similarly gathered together and bound near the end for a space of 2 inches. The lock from the center of the tonsure is included in this binding.

The following description of the scalp shown in d, is quoted from our previous report:[1] " A ' part ' 1 inch wide, from which the hair has been clipped, runs up to a large semilunar tonsure at the crown. The brow tresses on either side are gathered together in ' bobs ' that fall in front of or over the ears, and are tied up with wrappings of apocynum (?) string. The long hair from just behind the tonsure is braided into a thin plait, the lower end of which is doubled back on itself and bound with hair string. The remainder of the back hair is made into a single short thick ' bob,' string-wrapped, that falls to the nape of the neck." As shown in the drawing this specimen combines features of both figures b and c, but is more elaborate than either. It seems to have been preserved as a trophy and for this reason, when discussing it in the earlier report, we were in doubt as to whether it represented a method of hair-dressing practised by the Basket-makers, or that of some tribe of which we had no knowledge. The side-bobs inclined us to the belief that it was a Basket-maker style, as Basket-maker pictographs are often shown with " bobs " on either side of the head. The finds from White Dog Cave serve of course to confirm this idea.

Although many tribes shaved one portion or another of the head, and the thin scalp-lock was not an unusual thing, we can find no reference to analogous coiffures ancient or modern with the exception of those of the Maya thus described by Bishop Landa:

They wore their hair long, like women. On the top they burned a sort of tonsure; they let the hair grow around it, while the hair of the tonsure remained short. They bound the hair in braids about the head with the exception of one lock, which they allowed to hang down behind like a tassel.[2]

Judging from our material it would seem that the men dressed their hair more elaborately than did the women.

[1] Kidder-Guernsey, 1919, p. 191.   [2] Schellhas, 1904, p. 617.

CRADLES AND ACCESSORIES

Rigid Cradles. It seems well, before taking up the several empty cradles in the collection, to describe the one case in which we have the baby with all its wrappings still in place. The bundle is shown as found in plate 4, g, and plate 21, c; its different parts are separated and spread out in the other figures of the former plate. The infant, enveloped in robes, is tied in by means of a criss-cross lashing. The binding cord is of human hair, four-ply and 5 feet long (plate 4, i); it is rove through a series of string loops that are attached to the sides of the cradle. The seven stout cords that may be seen hanging loose on the left side of the unwrapped bundle (plate 4, g and plate 21, c), and laid out separately in h, had probably been used for hanging up or transporting the cradle; if the baby had not died so soon (it can hardly be more than a few days old), these cords would undoubtedly have been woven into a regular carrying strap like those shown in plate 23, k, l.

The outermost wrapping is a much tattered remnant of woven cloth (plate 4, a); it is described on page 63. The second cover is a fur-string baby blanket, measuring 17 by 17 inches. The body of the robe is of cords overlaid with strips of rabbit skin, its outer sides have a border, two strands in width, made of string, between the plies of which are caught bunches of long, coarse hair, probably dog. We have called coverings of this sort baby blankets because they were obviously woven to their peculiar bifurcated shape for the special purpose of leaving an opening at the place where they would otherwise constantly have been wet and soiled. Inside this blanket there was another of exactly the same size and shape; (plate 4, f) but, because it was to hold the baby itself, much softer and more carefully made. It is also of string, wound with strips of fluffy white fur from the bellies of rabbits. In handling this specimen, one is so impressed by the freshness of the fur that it is difficult to reconcile its perfect condition to its great antiquity.

The mummy of the infant (plate 4, c) lay on this inner blanket with the lower side-pieces folded over its legs. It was provided with a loose bundle of shredded cedar bark to serve as a diaper (e). On the abdomen, covering the navel, was a pad (d), made of cedar bark sewed up in prairie-dog skin, the hair side out. This obviously acted as a binder to prevent rupture. The umbilical

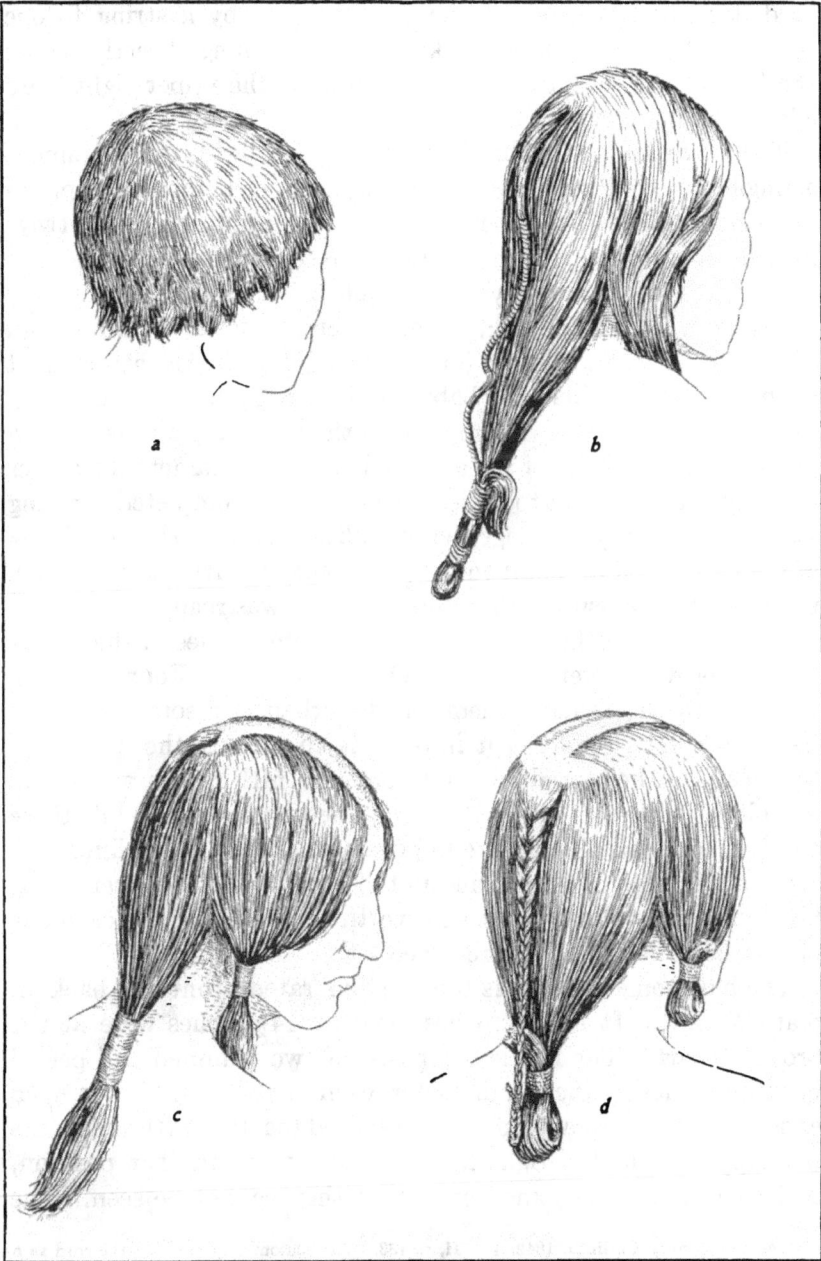

Styles of hair-dressing as shown by the remains from Basket-maker caves.

cord itself had been dried and was attached by a string to one corner of the outer baby blanket, so that it hung directly before the face of the infant;[1] it may be seen at the upper right-hand edge of the blanket (b).

The cradle (i) is 14 inches long and 10 inches wide. The frame is a single unpeeled withe, $\frac{1}{2}$ inch in diameter, bent into an approximate oval. The body is made of fifty straight, unpeeled twigs placed close together; these run transversely and are fastened underneath the frame by a continuous lashing of fiber string. Along each side of the cradle there extends a stout cord, fastened to the hoop at intervals and forming loose loops for the attachment of the binder that held the baby and its wrappings in place.

This cradle is much the smallest in the collection and is crudely made. It shows none of the careful finish and ornamental features of the specimens about to be described. The uncompleted carrying strap, the roughly put-together umbilical pad and the small size of the baby itself all point to the probability of birth having taken place before the usual elaborate " layette " was ready.

There are five other more or less complete cradles in the collection, all of which were found in White Dog Cave. Four had been buried with babies upon them but disturbance in some cases and decay in others rendered it impossible to recover the " mummy bundles " in their original condition; the fifth cradle was found in rude Cist 54 (plate 5, a) that contained no bones. While these specimens are all much alike in general make-up, they differ considerably in details. As no account of a rigid Basket-maker cradle has yet been published, it seems worth while to describe each one of this exceptionally well-preserved lot.

The handsomest cradle is the one illustrated, front and back, in plate 20, a, b. It is $23\frac{1}{2}$ inches long, by $14\frac{1}{2}$ inches wide at the broadest part. The rim is composed of two trimmed and peeled hardwood sticks $\frac{1}{2}$ inch in diameter, each bent into a U; the open ends of the two U-shaped pieces are spliced together with their sides overlapping a little; tight ligatures hold them in that position, and so envelop the joined ends that they cannot be seen. The

---

[1] As recorded by Catlin in 1842, Vol. II, p. 133. The custom of preserving the cord as a charm was practised by many tribes, particularly those of the plains. The Ute, Dakota, Arapaho, and Gros Ventre enclosed the dried cord in more or less elaborate coverings of skin ornamented with quill or bead work and fashioned usually to represent reptiles. These were hung on the front of the cradle (see Kroeber, 1908, pp. 166, 167).

body of the cradle is made of two series of slim willow twigs, from which the bark has been scraped. The transverse rods are ninety-nine in number; they are laid as close together as they will fit and are fastened at their ends to the under side of the frame by a continuous figure-eight lashing of yucca string. This binding is over-wrapped with soft fiber, until the slightly protruding ends of the rods are entirely hidden, and each side of the cradle is built up into a soft, bolster-like roll an inch in thickness; this in turn is sewed up in a cover of deer or mountain-sheep hide dressed with the hair on. The hard sides of the hoop and the sharp projecting rod ends are thus completely padded and form a sort of rim along the two edges of the cradle on its upper surface.

The second, or longitudinal, set of rods consists of five twigs running up the middle of the transverse rods and attached to them by a lashing of heavy sinew, so arranged as to produce the zigzag design seen in the photograph. The ends of the longitudinal twigs are fastened to the head and foot of the hoop in some manner which cannot be made out, because the attachment is padded and tightly sewed up in a hide covering.

Tied around the bottom of the hoop there is a horse-shoe shaped roll of cedar bark, which must have formed a kind of soft platform for the baby's feet to rest against when the cradle was held upright. A series of human hair strings are caught into the "bolsters" along the sides of the cradle; these, like the loops on the specimens first described, were to hold the laced binding cord. At the head and foot are much longer loops, designed, apparently, for suspending the cradle in a horizontal position.[1]

A double yucca string is tightly stretched across the upper surface of the cradle about 8 inches above the foot. From just below this string to the foot, the cradle is much discolored by the excreta of the baby. The purpose of the string was probably to hold in place the rather inefficient diaper-bundles of cedar bark or fiber.

Plate 20, c, d, illustrates a cradle very similar in shape to the above; its measurements, 23½ by 14¼ inches, are almost identical; the hoop is also made of two pieces tied together at the sides. The backing is of reeds instead of twigs; there are eighty-three in the transverse series and twenty-two in the longitudinal, the latter is secured to the former by narrow rawhide thongs whose emergences

[1] See Saunders, 1912, photograph facing p. 86.

75

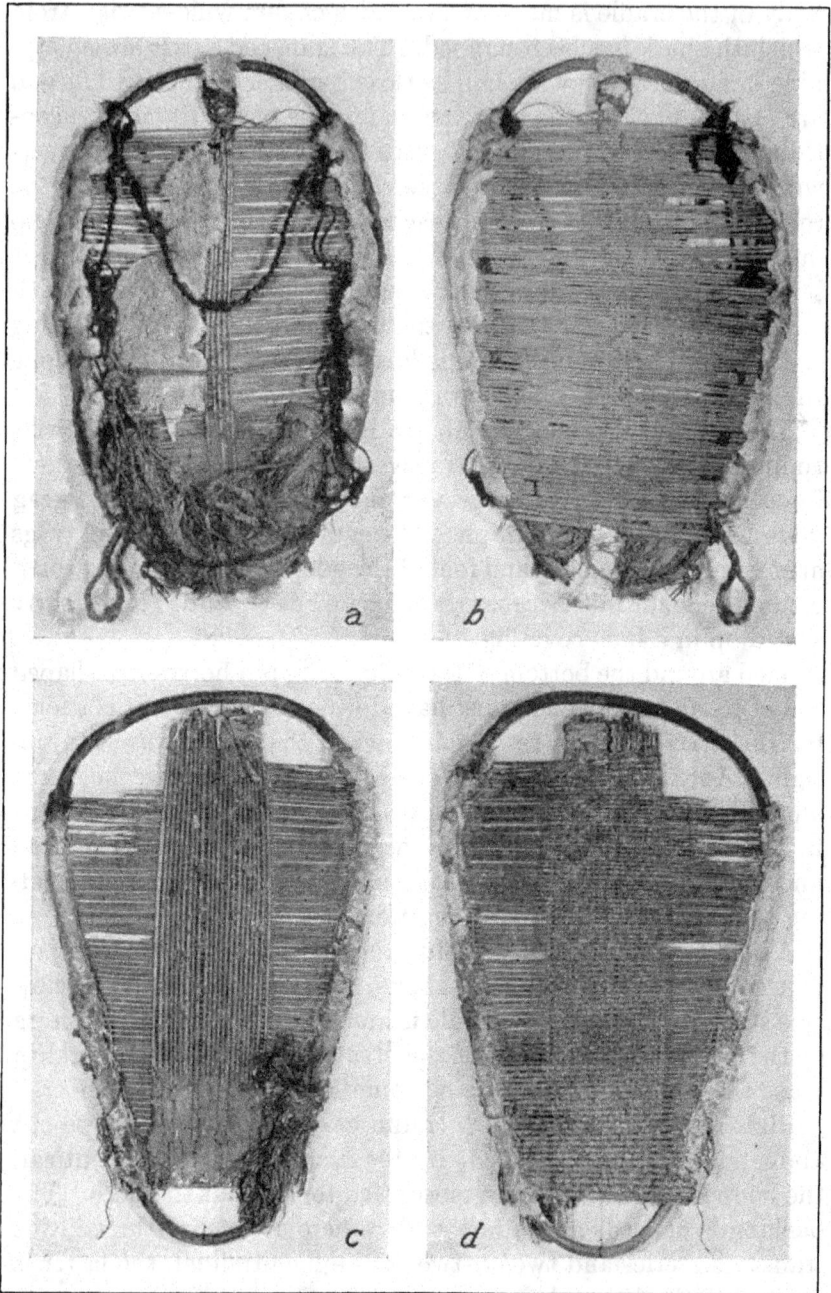

WHITE DOG CAVE

a, b, Front and back of cradle, Cist 35; c, d, Front and back of cradle, Cist 54. (About 1/9.)

produce a pattern of diamond figures. The longitudinal reeds were once attached to the head and foot of the bow, but their ends are now missing. The sides are padded with fiber and covered with hide, and there are the remnants of a cedar-bark foot rest. The ends of a diaper string are present, but there are no side loops for the laced binding cord.

The remaining three specimens are more nearly oval than the two preceding. The largest one (plate 21, b) is 25 inches long by 12 inches wide. Viewed from the side it is rocker-shaped, but this curve is probably due to warping. The frame and its side-padding (mostly decayed) offer no new features, nor does the method of attachment of the seventy-nine transverse willow backing-rods. As will be seen in the plate, the longitudinal rods are differently arranged; they are in two sets of six each, spaced well apart and curving away from each other as they approach the head of the cradle where each set is bent about the side of the frame and tied back on itself; the lower attachments are gone. The diamond-pattern lashings that hold the longitudinal to the transverse rods are of strips of rawhide. Between the two longitudinal sets, and also alongside them, the transverse rods are bound together by a sort of over-eight-under-eight twilling of leather thongs painted red. Side loops and diaper string have disappeared; the mark of the latter, however, can be made out on the backing, and below it there are as usual heavy stains and caked mud.

The cradle shown in plate 21, a, is from the same cist as the foregoing. It is an elongated oval, 19½ by 10½ inches. Of the two sticks bent to form its frame, the upper one is peeled, the lower unpeeled. The sides are padded into the usual long rolls, but there is no evidence that they were ever encased in skin; no loops or diaper string remain. The transverse twigs are ninety-eight in number; the first seventeen, counting from the top, are in natural color; then comes a row of eight rods dyed black, then eight in natural color, eight black, eight natural, eight black, eight natural, and eight black; the last twenty-five to the bottom are undyed. The eight longitudinal twigs are not attached to the transverse ones by the usual ornamental bindings. They are turned about the frame at the head of the cradle and tied back on themselves; at the bottom they are cut off at the level of the last transverse element and their ends are made fast to it by a row of twined yucca string.

The last of the three oval cradles is $21\frac{1}{2}$ inches long, and $11\frac{1}{4}$ inches across. The two sticks of its frame are unpeeled. There are seventy-seven transverse rods (willow twigs, scraped and trimmed as usual) and seven longitudinal ones, bound to the former with the conventional diamond pattern of thong-emergences; their attachments to the top and bottom of the frame have been broken off. The frame padding along the sides is of string and yucca fiber, and was once encased in hide. There are no side-loops, but the diaper string is still in place, stretched tightly across the upper surface of the cradle at a point one-third of the distance from the head to the foot.

Flexible Cradles. These are of two types. The first has a rim made of a long thin bundle of grass rolled tight, tied with yucca leaves and bent to the same shape as the wooden hoop of the rigid cradle. The body or filling is a rough mesh of yucca leaves. The second type is a sort of mat made from long strips of cedar bark held together by twined-woven rows of yucca leaves; the edges of the mat are turned up and fastened together by a yucca network. Both types are illustrated and more fully described in the report on the 1914–1915 expeditions;[1] all the specimens recovered in 1916–1917 were very fragmentary, but enough of them were found to show that these cradles were in common use.

Umbilical Pads. During the early part of the 1916 season there were taken from the graves of infants a number of flat pads, made by sewing up various substances in covers of prairie-dog hide. Their use, at first doubtful, was made clear when the well-preserved baby burial from Cist 13 was examined, and a similar pad (plate 4, d) was found lying against the navel of the infant; a second case (infant from Cist 35) was discovered later. It was then obvious that all these specimens had been used as are our modern " binders" to prevent umbilical hernia by exerting pressure on the navel of the new-born child.

Each of these pads has a light but rigid or semi-rigid core, most commonly made of five or six corncobs cut to equal length and bound together side by side; several examples are whittled from slabs of yellow-pine bark (plate 22, c);[2] still others consist of a rope or tight twist of cedar bark, coiled and sewed to itself to form

[1] Kidder-Guernsey, 1919, pp. 165, 166; plates 71, b; 72, a, b.
[2] The piece of bark figured in our first report (Kidder-Guernsey, 1919, plate 85, b), and classed as problematical is one of these.

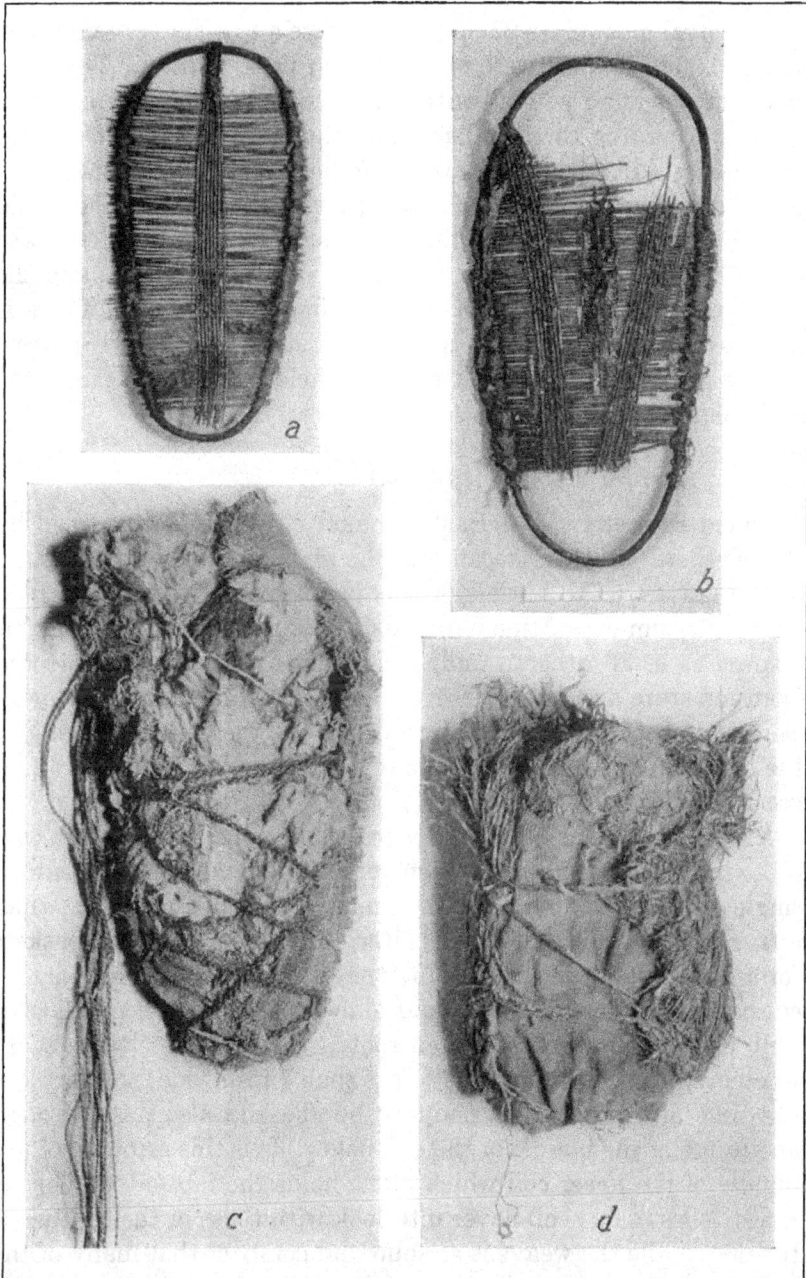

WHITE DOG CAVE

a, b, Cradles; c, Cradle containing mummy of child, Cist 13; d, Package containing
mummy of child, Cist 35. (About 1/10.)

a small oval mat (plate 22, b); in one case a thin slab of sandstone is used.[1] The crudest were wads of cedar bark or grass. The cores were wrapped and padded with shredded cedar bark, more or less thickly according to their hardness, and were finally enclosed in prairie-dog skin covers prepared as follows (plate 22, a); the complete hide was trimmed by cutting away the feet and tail, and shaped into a long bag with the fur outside. The padded core was placed in the bottom of this, the upper part folded down, and the whole neatly sewed up with sinew or fine fiber thread. There is one specimen (plate 31, a) to which is still attached the narrow human hair string band that formerly held it in place against the abdomen of the infant.

BASKETRY

Coiled Basketry. The Basket-maker culture was so named by the Wetherill brothers because of the abundance of baskets found in the graves. The burials of this people excavated by the Peabody Museum expeditions in Marsh Pass ran true to type in this respect as in all others; and, wherever the cists were protected from moisture and undisturbed by ancient looters, fine specimens were always to be found, while throughout the general digging in the caves fragments of worn-out baskets were encountered in great abundance.

All the specimens recovered were of the coiled variety, no case of twining, checkerwork, or wickerwork having been found; a single twilled example, in reality more like a flexible pouch than a true basket, will be described later. In weave the coiled baskets form a very homogeneous group; they are made over a foundation consisting of two slim osiers laid side by side, with a padding or welt of yucca fiber or shredded roots. The sewing elements are wooden splints averaging a little less than ⅛ inch wide; they enclose the rods and the fibrous padding bundle and also pass through about half of the bundle of the coil below. It is this gripping of the bundle of the lower coil which alone holds the fabric together, as the stitches of one coil never interlock with those of the coil below them.[2] While the weave is so solid and compact that many of the

---

[1] For a description of this specimen see Kidder-Guernsey, 1919, p. 192; its use was then unknown to us.

[2] For a diagram of the weave, see Kidder-Guernsey, 1919, figure 80.

better pieces must have been watertight, it never attains the fineness of texture seen in many California coiled baskets. These ancient weavers strove, apparently, for strength and serviceability rather than for refinement of technic. No more stitches than necessary were used; hence the relatively great width of the individual sewing splints and their broad spacing, which allows the foundation to appear between them. The average tray basket has five coils to the inch and nine to eleven stitches along each inch of coil; the finest specimen has eight coils and twelve stitches; the coarsest, a fragment from a large pannier, has coils $\frac{1}{2}$ inch wide and six to seven stitches to the inch of coil. The edge bindings of all the baskets save one are in simple wrapping; the exception is a bowl-shaped piece (plate 23, i) in which the entire rim is finished in " false-braid " as in Navajo baskets.[1]

Our specimens fall into the following five classes:

1. Trays   4. Water baskets
2. Bowls   5. Trinket baskets
3. Carrying baskets

Trays. This is by far the commonest type. The examples are very flat, and run from 12 to 24 inches in diameter. They were probably used for the serving of food, and perhaps in gambling. One tray (plate 23, j) obviously had another purpose; about its rim at equal distances apart were four loops, two of which remain (the others were in place when found, but soon crumbled away). Each loop is made of a twig tied into a circle 2 inches in diameter and is attached to the rim of the basket by a short buckskin thong. The whole interior of the tray shows much wear, particularly severe at the bottom where, indeed, it had begun to give out and was re-enforced by overstitching with new splints, which themselves were partly worn through. The outside and bottom exhibit no wear at all. It seems likely that this basket was suspended by the loops and used for the simultaneous hulling and winnowing of seeds too delicate to be shelled in a mortar. The process might have been to keep a stone rolling among the seeds by shaking the suspended tray, and to blow off the hulls as they were detached by

---

[1] For details of this stitch, see Mason, 1904, figure 197. A Basket-maker basket from Grand Gulch, in which the last inch of the terminal coil is done in "false-braid" is mentioned by Pepper (1902, p. 16); exactly the same treatment appears in a basket from Step House, Mesa Verde (Nordenskiold, 1893, plate XLIV, 4); Diegueño and Kawia (southern California) tray baskets also have the last inch of coil in "false-braid" (Peabody Museum Collections).

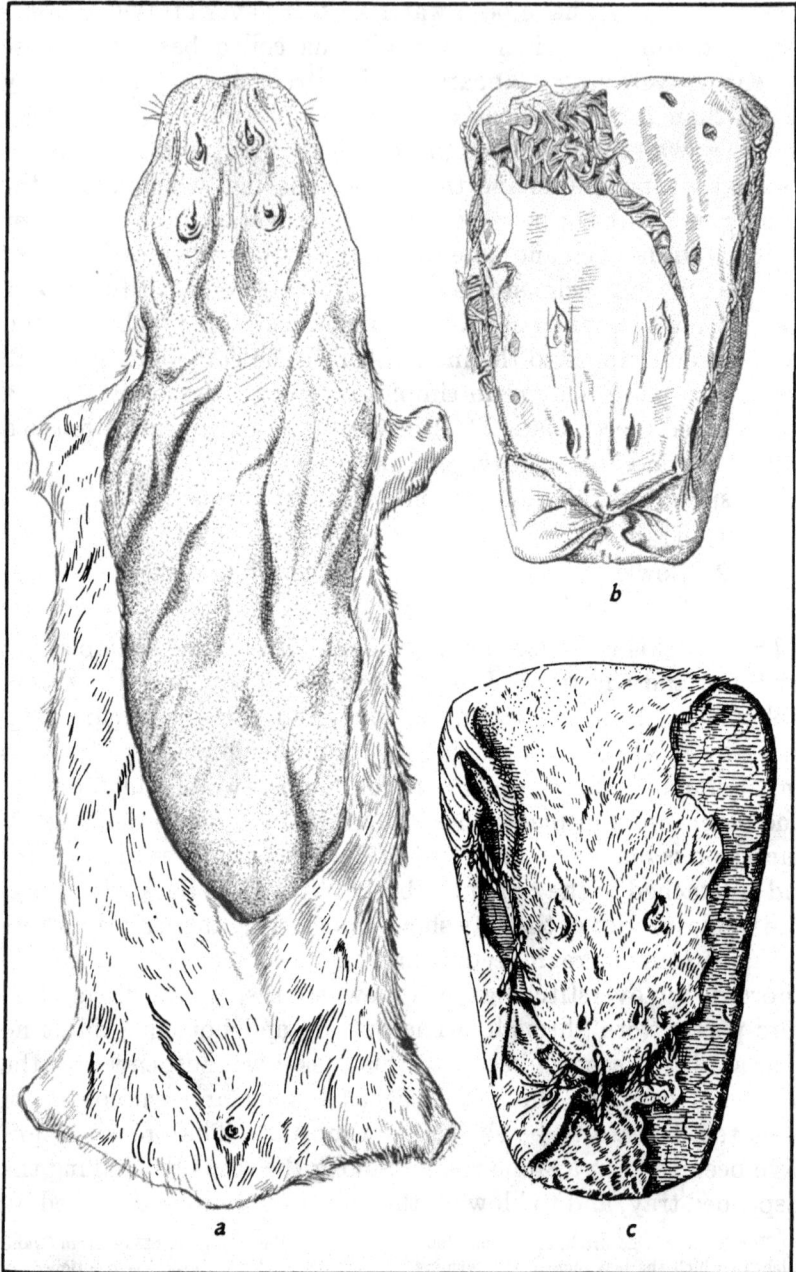

WHITE DOG CAVE
a, Covering for umbilical pad; b, c, Umbilical pads.   (About ⅜.)

the bruising of the stone. This explanation is, of course, pure guesswork, but it seems to account satisfactorily for the presence of the loops and for the excessive wear on the inside.

Bowls. As will be seen in the illustrations (plate 23, a, c, f) these baskets are of lesser diameter than the trays and of much greater depth; their bottoms are flat and the sides rise more or less steeply. The largest is 14 inches wide at the mouth, by 8 inches deep. We believe that some of the larger bowls were used for boiling by the hot stone method, as two examples are heavily daubed with a mixture of mud and ashes applied, apparently, to render them watertight; they also have a soiled and battered look and many patches that indicate hard use.

Carrying Baskets. These are the largest of the coiled baskets, measuring 28 to 30 inches in diameter at the top, by 17 to 20 inches deep. They have pointed bottoms, oval in cross-section; and widely flaring upper parts (plate 23, k, l). By actual count of coils and stitches to the inch these are the coarsest of the baskets, yet they are as carefully and regularly woven as the finest; are very strong, but flexible enough to adapt themselves to the curves of the neck and shoulders of their bearers. There is no doubt that they served as panniers for carrying loads on the back; their shape and the use of similar forms by modern tribes are sufficient indications. The identification, however, is rendered certain by the fact that they all have pairs of loops, usually of human hair string, worked into their sides at the proper height for the attachment of head bands. In two specimens these bands are still in place. The common use of these panniers to cover interments is, of course, a secondary one.

Water Baskets. The excavations of 1916–1917 produced no whole specimen of this type, yet fragments of oval bottoms of a finer weave than is usual in panniers seem to indicate that such baskets were not rare. A fine example from Cave II, Kinboko, is figured in our former report. Dimensions: total height 17 inches, greatest diameter $14\frac{3}{4}$ inches, orifice $4\frac{1}{2}$ inches. It has an elongated base, oval in cross-section. The upper part flares out and becomes round; it is constricted again at the top, and the orifice is small. There does not seem to have been a neck, but there is some evidence that there was once a string-hinged cover. On opposite sides, just below the point of greatest diameter, are pairs of carrying loops made by twisting into a heavy cord eight or ten two-strand human hair strings. The entire inner surface of the basket is thickly pitched with piñon gum, and the same material has been daubed on such parts of the exterior as had begun to wear through. A design of small stepped units may be faintly made out on the upper curve.[1]

Trinket Baskets. These are neatly made little receptacles with round bodies and small orifices. The range of sizes and shapes is shown in the illustrations (plates 23, h, and 24, d). It is probable that these baskets were put to a variety of uses; many of those found in the graves contained small trinkets of one sort or another.

Decoration. Baskets of all the above types were ornamented with designs in black. Red elements, reported by Pepper[2] in Grand Gulch baskets, are not found in our collection. The designs are of great interest because they are without much doubt the oldest examples of basketry ornamentation that have yet come to light in the United States. Furthermore, they illustrate the decorative art of a people who preceded the pottery-making tribes of the region, and so may eventually be expected to throw light on the vexed question of whether or not southwestern pottery designs developed from those of basketry. We give, accordingly, all the decorations that are sufficiently well-preserved to copy (plate 24). These, together with the fine series of baskets figured by Pepper,[3] will give the reader a very good idea of the make-up of the designs. Descriptions of the patterns tell no more than do the pictures, and any attempt to supply symbolical meanings to designs as old as these would naturally be pure guesswork. We have made notes towards a comparative study of these and the designs of the baskets from the Plateau and Pacific Coast areas, but they are as yet far from complete, nor have we space in this publication to present the mass of data which has already accumulated. It may be said, however, that the art as a whole seems to find its nearest parallel in that of the central and northern California tribes. In technic, on the other hand, the baskets most closely resemble those of the Paiute.

[1] Kidder-Guernsey, 1919, p. 170 and plate 78.
[2] 1902, p. 15.
[3] Ibid., the same pictures may also be found in Mason, 1904, a more accessible publication, plates 84, 104, and 205 to 211 inclusive.

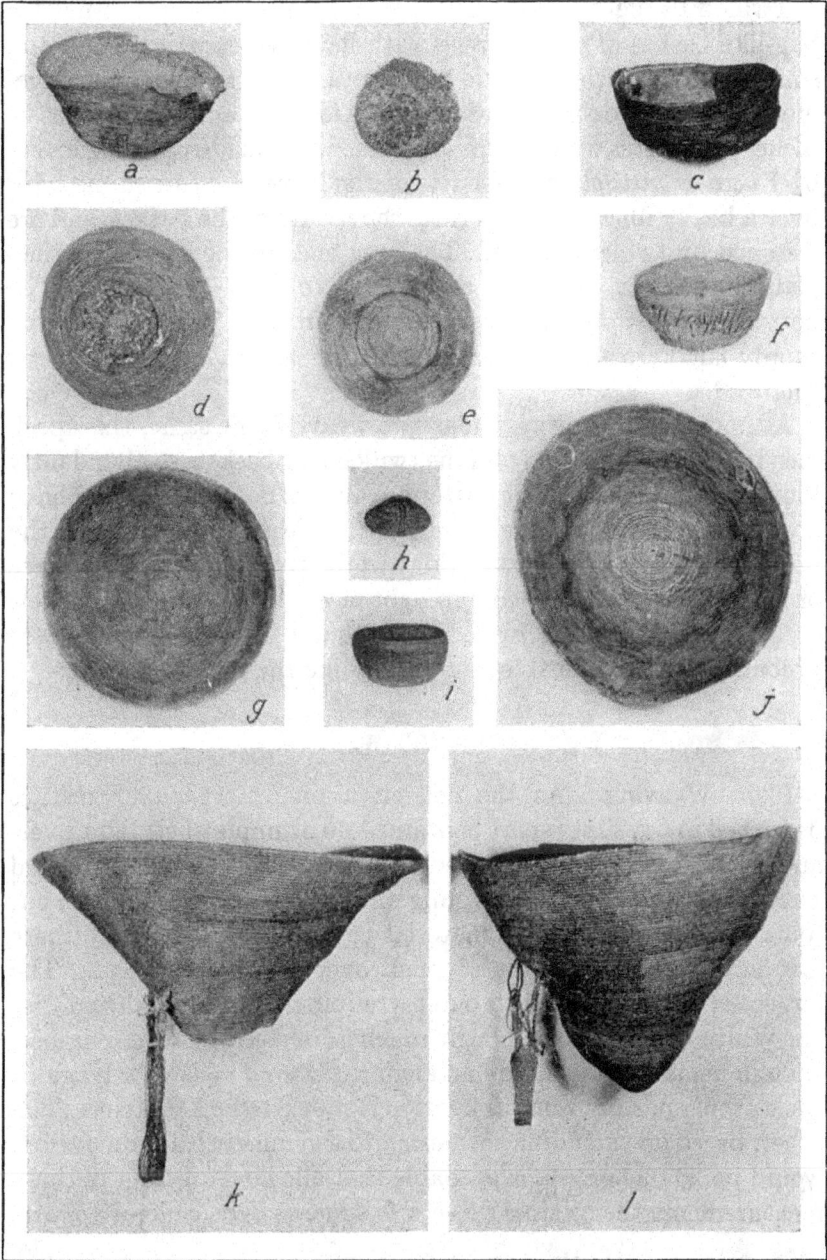

Baskets: All from White Dog Cave with the exception of h, which is from Cave 1,
Kinboko Canyon, Marsh Pass. (About 1/16.)

Twilled Basketry. The only specimen in this weave is a flexible bag-like basket of yucca leaves with flattened spherical body and small mouth. Although it is fragmentary, the following measurements are approximately correct: width 8½ inches; depth 4½ inches; diameter of aperture 4 inches. It is made of entire leaves of *Yucca angustifolia;* the butts of the leaves are turned outward over a heavy fiber cord that rings the mouth of the basket, and are fastened by twined strings. The long ends of the leaves are then plaited together, over-two-under-two, to form the body. The bottom is not woven, the last couple of inches of the leaves being simply laid across each other and tied in that position with string (plate 23, b).

Although the over-two-under-two weave is the same, this specimen is entirely different from the twilled ring baskets so abundantly found in cliff-houses.[1] The latter are always bowl-shaped and have a wooden hoop at the edge. They are fabricated upwards from the bottom; not, as in this case, downwards from the rim. No trace of ring baskets has yet come to light in our excavations in Basket-maker caves; a bit of twilled work found in Cave 1, 1915,[2] was probably part of a flexible bag-basket like the present one.

TEXTILES

Plain Weaving. As the collection of Basket-maker textiles described in our first report contained no example of straight over-and-under weaving, we believed that the Basket-makers practised but two technics, namely twining and coiled-netting (coil without foundation). Among the material collected in 1916–1917 there are, however, three pieces of plain over-and-under weave. The largest of these is the cloth outer wrapping of the infant from Cist 13, White Dog Cave. Though much torn and showing long use, enough remains so that by arranging tattered ends of selvage in their proper positions one dimension is shown to be 27½ inches. The other, based on extending the design to a symmetrical termination, would be 26 inches. It is probable that allowing for error in these measurements the original piece was square. The general appear-

---

[1] See Kidder-Guernsey, 1919, p. 108 and plate 43. The specimens figured by Pepper (1902, p. 23) are probably not Basket-maker, particularly as one of them was found filled with beans; the basket shown on p. 25, however, seems to be identical with the one under discussion.

[2] Kidder-Guernsey, 1919, p. 167.

ance of the fabric is the same as that of the twined-woven bags both in color and design, the difference in technic not being apparent at first sight. The weave is rather coarse, having nine warp and fifteen weft strands to the inch. Both warp and weft are of a uniform sized two-strand twist of rather coarse vegetal fiber presumably yucca. As far as it is possible to work it out from the scant material at hand the weave is as shown in the diagrammatic drawing, figure 11, b. Details as to the manner in which the warp edge is finished appear in figure 11, b, and plate 25, c. The warp ends are cut close and the weft kept from unraveling by a buttonhole stitch. The edge running parallel to the warp is finished by twining two fine strands of human hair through the loops that result from turning back the weft for a new start; this also is illustrated in figure 11, b.

In the photograph, plate 4, a, there is seen at one point a circular hole, cut in the fabric, and finished all around by overcasting with fiber thread. The design (plate 26, b) consists of a series of large rectangles arranged in three rows, the two outside rows red, the center one black. The units average 2½ inches long by 1½ inches wide. Separately dyed elements were not introduced to produce the design; but apparently, when the weaving reached a point where a change of color was desired, the weft strand was thoroughly rubbed with color for the required length and then woven in. The warp cords show little color, such as appears on them probably resulting from contact with the weft. It is possible that the finished piece may have been treated with some mordant to fix the dye.

The second example of this weave is a fragment 12 inches long by 2 inches wide in very bad condition, one end showing darning. It is also from White Dog Cave. There are traces of a broad design in red, the exact character of which cannot be determined. The piece appears to be a part of a blanket very similar to the one just described. There remains a short section of one edge finished with a thread of human hair twined through the weft loops.

The third piece, from Cave 11, Sagiotsosi, was found with the disturbed burial described on page 37. It is very evenly woven with fourteen warp and twenty-one weft strands to the inch. The fragment has a length one way of 12 inches, and is a part of one corner of the original piece, so that two edges remain. Both warp and weft edges are finished in the same manner as the one first de-

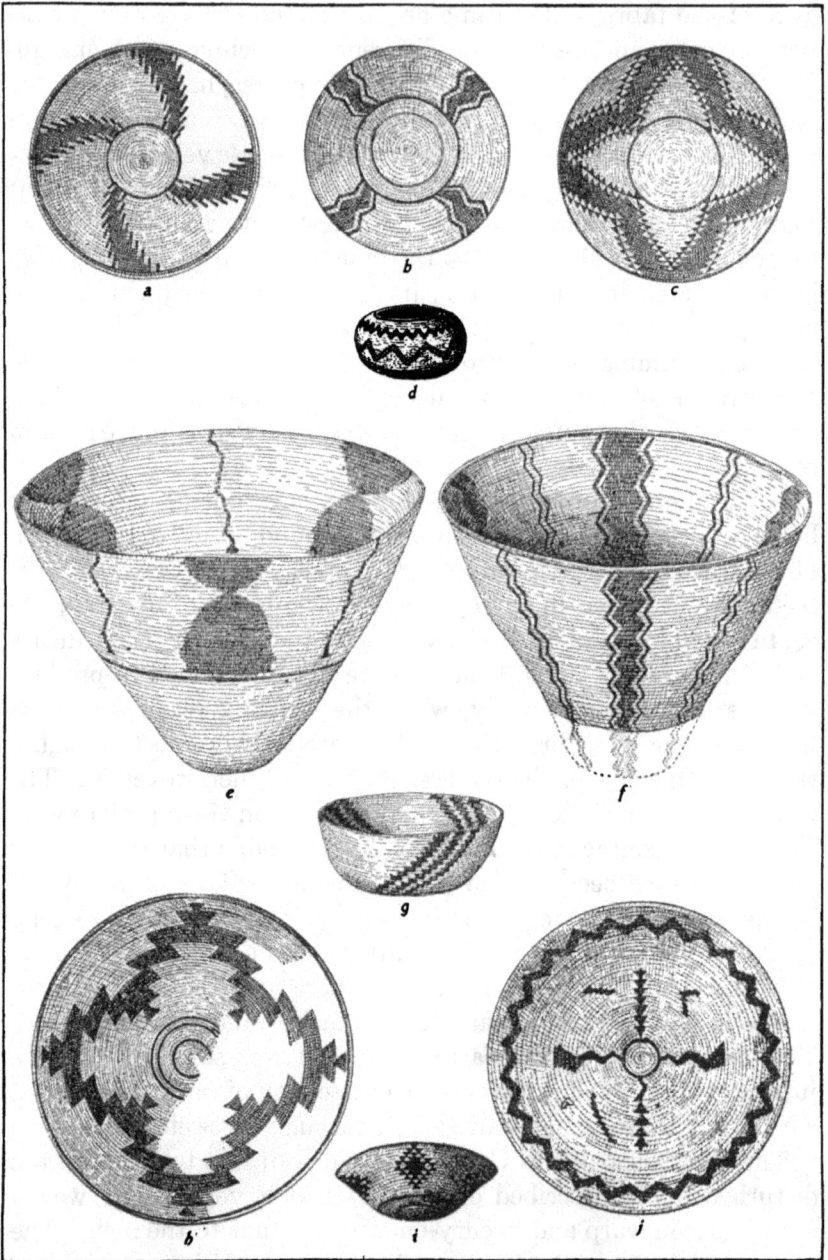

Baskets: All from White Dog Cave with the exception of d, which is from Cave 2,
Kinboko Canyon, Marsh Pass.   (About 1/16.)

scribed: a buttonhole stitch of fine string, and human hair twining thread respectively. The design is in red and black, and so far as it can be traced is shown in plate 26, c. It is painted, not woven, and the color was applied only to one side of the cloth; the red pigment has soaked through the fabric and the red parts of the design appear faintly on the back. The black paint has not soaked through at all. To the corner is tied a dressed leather thong, which leads us to think that it may have been part of a garment.

These fabrics remind one strongly of the Coahuila cave textiles, many of which are large poncho-like blankets woven in the same

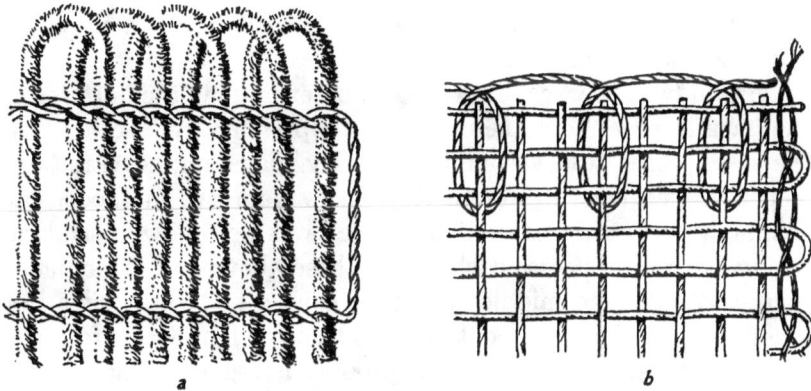

FIGURE 11

a, Detail of weave, fur cloth blankets; b, Plain woven cloth, detail of weave and selvage.

way as these, and also have one edge finished with the buttonhole stitch. The latter resemblance seems significant, since we have not been able to find in the Museum collection textiles from any other region so finished. The designs, it is true, are different, though some of the elements seen in the Basket-maker twined-woven bags are also found in the Coahuila blankets.

The zigzag lines seen in the second specimen (plate 26, c) are very similar to the zigzags painted on the breasts of certain square-shouldered Basket-maker pictographs from the Monuments.[1] This resemblance has suggested to us that these woven fabrics may have been used as shirts.

Twined Weaving. The bags illustrated on plates 26, 28, and 30 form one of the most interesting groups in the collection, not only

---

[1] Kidder-Guernsey, 1919, p. 197, figures 100, 101.

because of the excellence of their manufacture and the variety and beauty of their decoration, but also because they are so peculiarly characteristic of the Basket-maker culture. We have, fortunately, a large amount of material: complete bags to illustrate size, shape, and design; and great numbers of rags and fragments to make clear the details of technic.

The bags are flexible seamless sacks with full, round bodies and long, gradually constricted necks (plate 26, a, d). They range from 1½ inches to 2 feet or more in length. All are made in the same way, of close twined weaving; the majority of specimens have both warp and weft of two-ply apocynum string, though some have yucca warp and apocynum weft. The combination of apocynum warp and yucca weft is rare.

Our study of the weave was begun by examining the bottoms of the bags in order to make out how the preliminary " set-up " of the warp cords was accomplished. By dissecting several fragmentary specimens we found that there were two methods, one common, the other rare. The former was as follows: six long strands were laid across each other, three above and three below (figure 12, a); the middle strand of each set of three runs out straight, the others are bent so that their ends radiate from the common center. There are thus produced twelve original warps. The second method consists of twisting three strands about each other and then bending their ends so that they radiate and form six warp cords (figure 12, b).

The above systems are very simple and practical, and avoid the ugly lump and the potential weakness in the fabric which would have been the result of knotting the warps together at the base. The method of inserting the weft also obviates knotting: a single long string is worked over and under the radiating warp cords close about their common center; this is shown slack in figure 12, a, b; in reality it is pulled up very tight and holds the warp firmly together. When a circuit of the spoke-like warps has been made, the two ends of the weft string of course come together; they are then combined into a single strand of twined weaving, which continues spirally around and around to form the body of the bag fabric.

To return to the warp-skeleton. Many large bags have as many as three hundred and fifty warps at their point of greatest diameter.

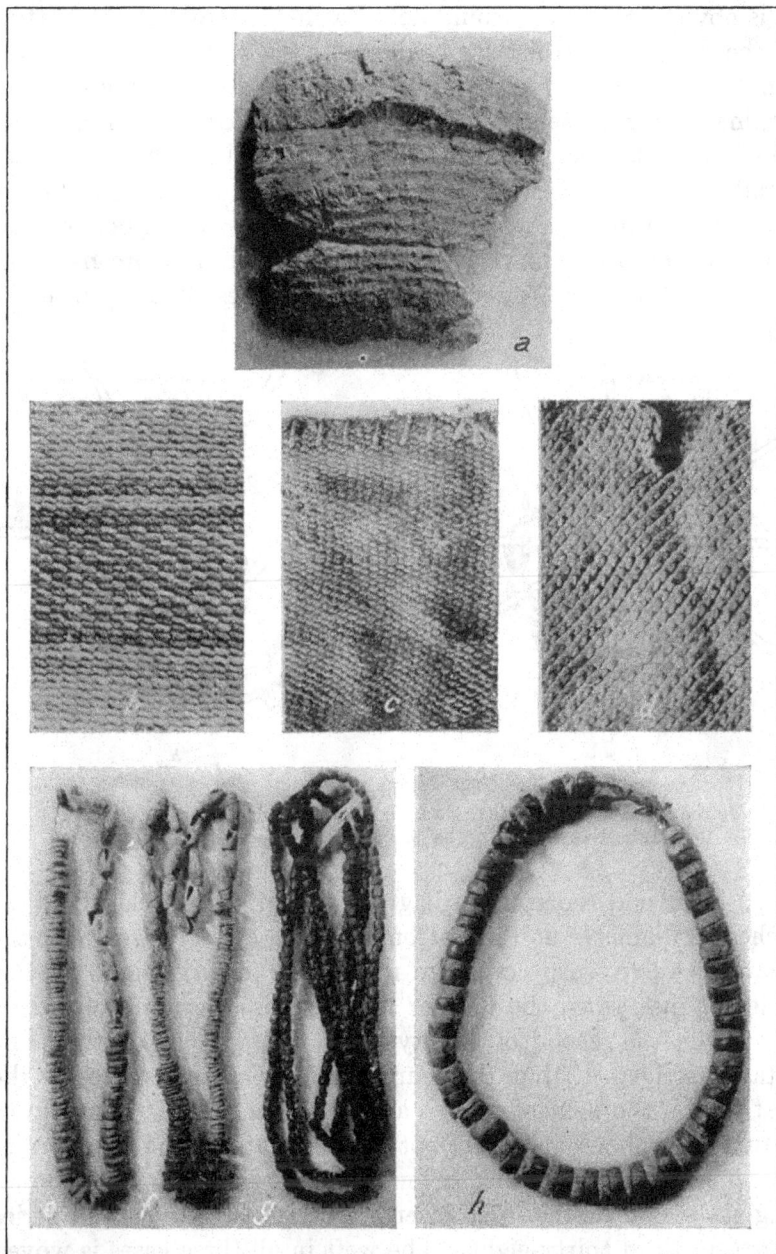

a, Pottery, Cave 6; b, Twined-woven fabric, White Dog Cave; c, Plain woven fabric, Sagiotsosi Canyon; d, Coiled netted fabric, White Dog Cave; e–h, Necklaces, White Dog Cave.

It is obvious that these could not all come together at the bottom of the bag; hence the base begins with six or twelve warps only (as described above) and sets of new cords are introduced as the original ones radiate away from each other. Upon the number of new warps depends the size of the finished bag; and upon the rapidity of their insertion depends the degree of flare imparted to the base. If many new warps are added close to the bottom, the latter will naturally be very flat; if they are put in more gradually the bag will have an egg-shaped base. Figures 13, a, b, illustrate

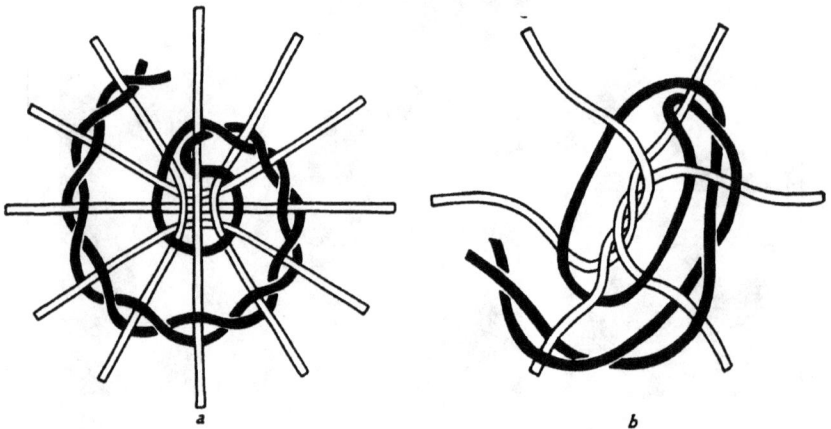

FIGURE 12

Methods of arranging and binding warp cords when beginning the construction of twined-woven bags. The weft cords are shown in solid black.

this; each one represents, diagrammatically, a circle about $1\frac{1}{2}$ inches in diameter at the bottom of a bag. In figure 13, a, the original twelve warp cords are multiplied to forty-eight by two series of insertions, the first or inner series consisting of twelve new cords, the second of twenty-four. In figure 13, b, the same total is arrived at, but there are three series of insertions; the first of six, the next of twelve and an outer one of twenty-four. Figure 13, c, shows an area of bottom no greater than in the former specimens, but containing seventy-six warps, set in as follows: original series twelve, first insertion series twelve, second series fourteen, third thirty-eight. The weft in all three cases is woven in with approximately the same degree of tightness; hence the warps of a and b are pulled close to each other and the bags have narrower bottoms than in c, where the quicker insertion of warps allows the base to grow rapidly broader.

We have not yet mentioned the actual method of inserting new warps. Two ways were employed. In one (plate 27, b) the string to be added was looped and laid between two of the old warps (b, b') thus forming two new ones (a, a'); the first two or three turns of the weft (c, c') attach the new strands to the old warps on either side of them holding all firmly in place; the next turn of weft (d) takes in each new element separately and the weaving continues normally.

In the second method (plate 27, a), the strand to be added was doubled into a loop, making, as before, two new warps; the string

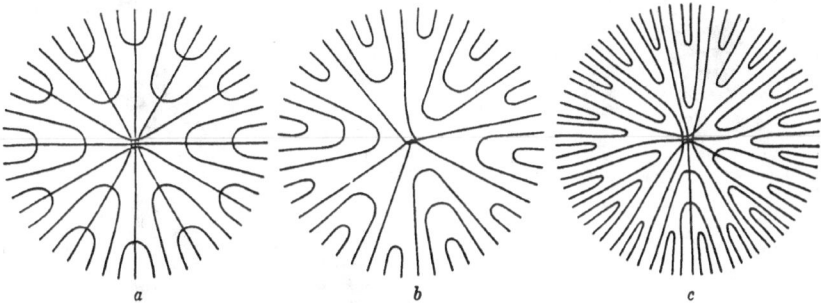

a   b   c

FIGURE 13

Methods of inserting new warp cords to increase diameter of bottom of bags.

at the bend of the loop was twisted apart into its two component plies and one of the old warps (b) was threaded through the resultant opening; the loop (a, a') was then slid up the old warp and brought close against the last woven turn of the weft (c), thus producing a pair of new warps (a, a') one on each side of the original one (b); on its next revolution about the bag the weft (d) takes in the two new warps and holds them solidly.

By the two methods just detailed the new warps become integral parts of the fabric without leaving any loose ends and without necessitating any disfiguring knots. The tension on the warps, however, incident to the use of the bags, tends to pull the loops very tight and so away from the last weft turn woven previously to their insertion, thus producing the little open space in the web indicated in the two figures. Where many new warp-pairs were introduced (as in the outer circle of figure 13, c) these little holes

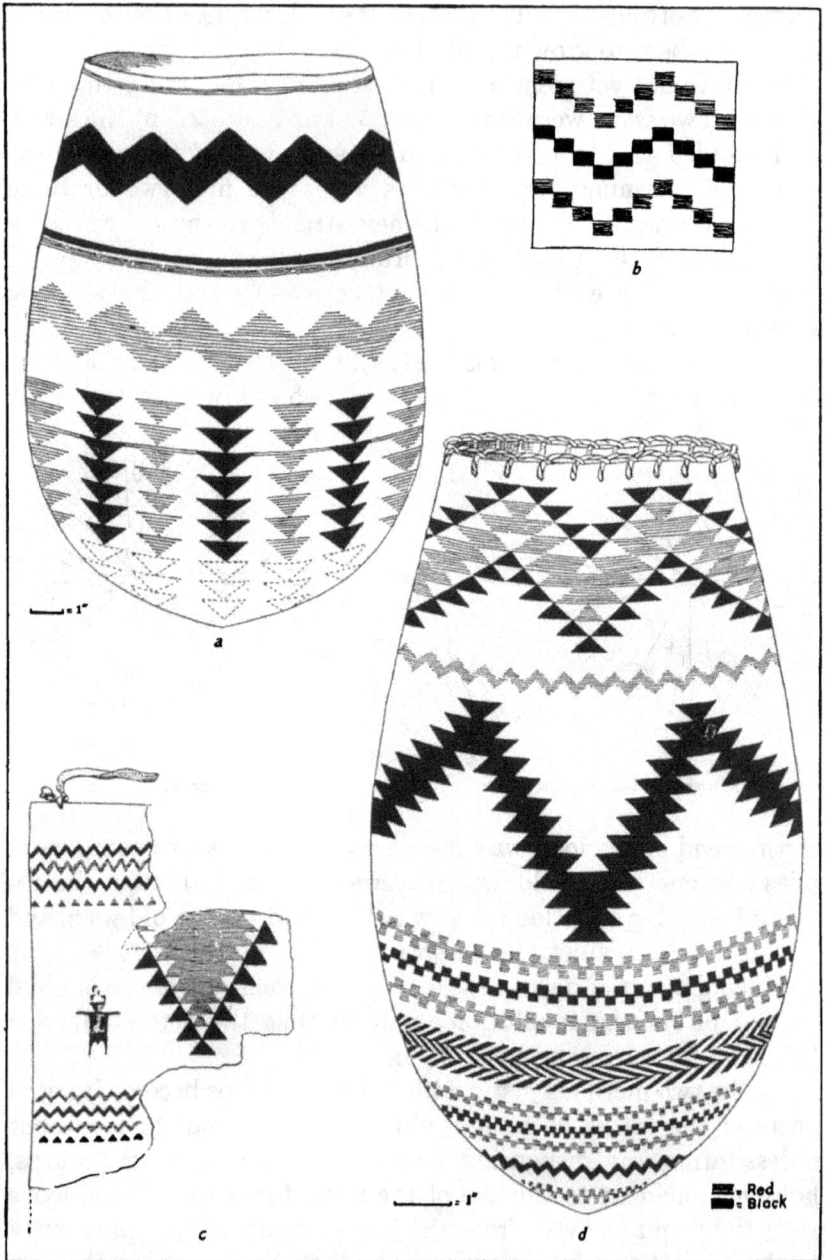

Textile designs: a d, Twined-woven bags; b, c, Plain woven cloth.

naturally lie close together and make very characteristic open-work rings about the bottoms of the bags.

The two different ways of adding warps (figure 13, a, b) are about equally common. In most bags either one or the other is adhered to; occasionally the two are mixed (figure 13, c). All bags seem to start with either six or twelve original warps, the ultimate size of the fabric depending on the number of new ones introduced; a medium-large bag (A–3054) had at its point of greatest diameter a total of about three hundred and fifty warps. Almost all specimens are more or less constricted toward the mouth; this is accomplished partly by tightening the twining of the weft and thus bringing the warp closer together, and partly by dropping out warps. A warp to be dropped is merely cut off and its end hidden by the next turn of the weft.

The final point in the study of the warps is the method of securing them at the edge or mouth of the bag to insure a strong and ravel-proof selvage. This was sometimes accomplished by turning the warp ends about a stout edge-string (figure 14, a) and running them back a little way on themselves; they were held in this position by the last few turns of the weft; their loops about the edge cord were then pulled tight and the ends of the cords clipped off close to the fabric. In other cases the warp ends were looped under each other, then gathered into bundles of four or five, tucked with an awl through the fabric just below the edge and finally clipped (figure 14, b). A third method also dispensed with the edge-cord: each warp was bent at the edge, paired with the warp next it, run back along it towards the bottom of the bag, held by the upper weft-turns, pulled snug, and clipped (figure 14, c).[1]

We now take up the twining of the weft, which is perfectly simple and regular. It begins at the very bottom (figure 12, a, b) and continues in a close spiral to the mouth. Fresh lengths of weft string were not tied to the ends of the old ones (these weavers seem to have had a deep-seated aversion to knots), but were run a little way with them until firmly set. The entire weft, while made, of course, of many pieces, is thus essentially continuous. The method of procedure is unknown; it is probable, however, that the work was downward, the base of the bag having been attached

---

[1] Compare with a similar method of fastening warp ends in Cliff-dweller sandal heels (Kidder-Guernsey, 1919, p. 104 and figure 38).

to a limb or pole and the warps allowed to hang either free or tied in loose bunches to prevent tangling.[1] The twelve-year old daughter of one of the authors has experimented with this technic and has quickly become expert in making the bags. She holds the two weft-strings loosely across the palm of her hand separated by the index finger and gives the twist necessary to cross them between warps by merely turning the hand over. Each successive warp is hooked up and drawn between the wefts with the index finger. No tool is necessary for beating up the weft, as it

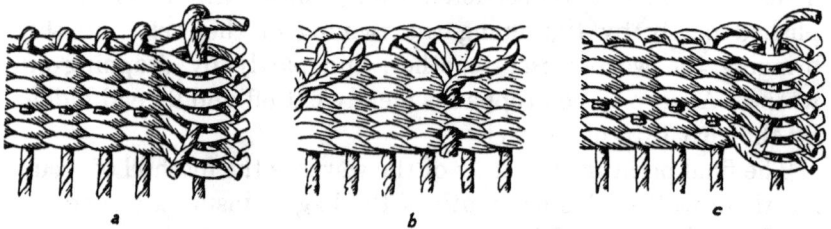

FIGURE 14
Various methods of finishing the top of twined-woven bags.

can be made to sit tightly by a slight pull after every few warp crossings.

The weave of the ancient specimens is very even, and the number of wefts per inch over the whole surface of any given bag is always practically the same, though the warps at the necks of constricted examples are pulled somewhat closer together than they are at the swell of the bodies. The coarsest weave in the collection (A–3005) has five warps and fourteen weft-pairs per square inch; the finest (A–3161) has fourteen warps and twenty-three weft-pairs. The normal texture lies approximately half way between these two extremes with about nine warps and seventeen or eighteen weft-pairs.

The decoration of the bags is no less interesting than their structure. There are two styles, woven and painted, both sometimes appearing on the same piece.

The woven ornaments were accomplished by what may be termed the " dyed weft " process. When a band of color was to be introduced a new weft-pair of the desired shade was not added,

[1] See a picture of a Virginia Indian woman weaving a bag-like basket, Mason, 1904, figure 148.

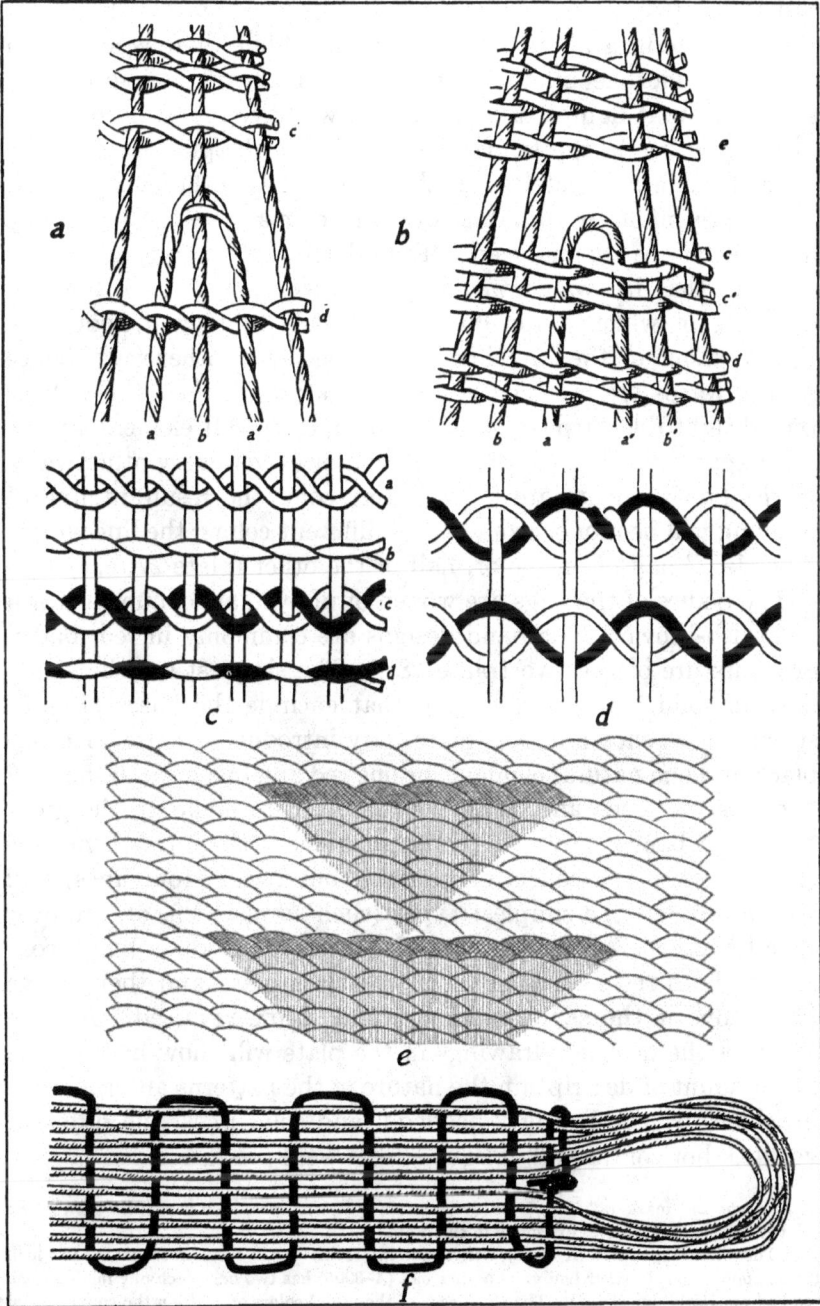

a–e, Details of twined-woven bags; f, Detail of plain woven carrying-strap.

but the weft then in use was itself stained or rubbed with dye for the requisite length and then woven in. While there is no reason why very short lengths of weft should not have been so colored and small unit figures thus produced, we have found no instance of the practice in the twined bags,[1] all the designs being in the form of bands completely encircling the bodies of the sacks. These bands are infinitely variable, but all are made in the same way and are very easily analyzed. To understand them one must keep in mind that in twined weaving a double weft is used, the two elements of which twine both about each other and about the warps. Each of the two elements crosses every other warp, hence all the warps are crossed (plate 27, c, a); and when the weft is pulled tight the warp is entirely hidden, each weft element (in the pair) appearing on the surface of the fabric over every other warp. If the two elements are of the same color the resultant line of weaving will be monochrome; if of different colors, the line will be " beaded," half of one color, half of the other (plate 27, c, d).

The bodies of the bags are woven of undyed apocynum, a warm yellowish-brown. The band designs are commonly in red, black, or a mixture of the two (plate 28).[2] The simplest are the single lines in solid black or solid red that encircle the bases of most specimens as shown in this plate. By introducing wefts with one black and one natural element, or one red and one natural, beaded lines are produced and these are combined to make up the great variety of bands shown in the illustrations. They are all narrow (the widest in the collection contains but twenty-four lines) and no two, except the simplest types (such as plate 29, c), are ever exactly alike. A favorite practice was to make a band containing both red and black as in b, of this plate, and then weave just above it the same band with the colors reversed. A little study of the detailed drawings in the plate will show better than any amount of description the nature of the patterns and the ways in which, by combining " beaded " and solid lines, the different vertical, horizontal and oblique effects were produced.

[1] Except as "markers" in painted designs (plate 27, e). See, however, the woven fabric (plate 26, b), where squares are made in this way.

[2] There is one specimen (A–3056) with a band in brown; this dye caused the string to which it was applied to rot rather badly. Another bag (A–3005) has two lines each one made of one red and one dark blue strand. The third case of the use of colors other than the conventional red and black, is the appearance of a few yellow lines in A–3470.

The type of pattern illustrated in e, is the only one which needs explanation. Normally the weave of the bags is counter-clockwise, and a series of " beaded " weft-rows produces an oblique design, whose lines run downward to the right as in a. By shifting the weave to a clockwise direction, the slant of the oblique lines is changed and they run downward to the left. The decoration shown in e, therefore, was made by introducing three clockwise rows, then six counter-clockwise, and finally six clockwise. There are but two examples of this style in the collection.

One further point should be noticed: the weft is continuous, going around and around the bag; if the number of warps were even, and if (for example) a weft-pair of one black and one natural strand were being used, the black strands would, at each successive revolution about the bag, cross the same warp, and a series of vertical black bars would be produced (as in the two upper rows of f). If on the other hand, the number of warps were odd, the emergences of the black strand on the surface would be offset at each revolution and the resultant design would be oblique as in a. As both types, vertical and oblique, often occur in the same band, as shown in d, it is obvious that when the change from oblique to vertical or vice versa was to be made the weaver had to employ some device to reverse the order of emergences of her alternating colors. How this was done is shown in plate 27, d.

Painting, the second style of bag decoration, would call for little notice beyond the illustration of the designs themselves, were it not for two very interesting peculiarities, namely, the practice of applying the designs to the inside as well as to the outside of the bags, and the use of markers woven in, apparently to aid in this duplication. These methods were employed in the decoration of the bag shown in plate 30, f, and restored in color in plate 28.

Perhaps the clearest way of presenting the technic is to describe the steps by which we arrived at an understanding of it. We had examined the bags a number of times and had always supposed, because the designs appeared on both sides of the fabric, that they had been woven in probably by means of the dyed-weft method; closer scrutiny, however, showed that the vertical and oblique edges of the figures were perfectly even and straight, not finely serrated or stepped as is always the case with such edges in a woven design. Under a magnifying glass the edges of the colored

WHITE DOG CAVE
Color-scheme of woven bag.

areas proved to be formed not by the stitches of the weave, but to run quite independently of them as illustrated in plate 27, e. This showed, of course, that the designs had been painted on, not woven in; but we were still at a loss to account for the accuracy with which they were reproduced on the reverse of the fabric (we had pushed pins through the weave at various juts and corners of the figures and had found that their points protruded at exactly corresponding places in the designs on the other side). We then decided that some dye must have been used which struck clear through the material and colored both surfaces. This explanation satisfied us until we chanced to pry apart some of the weft strings, and noticed that their under parts and the warps were not colored. This puzzled us greatly because we could not conceive of a dye which would act on both surfaces of a cloth without affecting its body. We then returned to our pin tests, and eventually discovered a few places where the designs on front and back failed to correspond by a small fraction of an inch, and one spot where there was an error of a quarter of an inch.

It was then clear that the two sides had been painted separately, but we could not understand how the elaborate patterns had been duplicated so exactly. Further examination cleared up this question also. We noticed that the top line of weaving in many of the colored units was of a darker shade than its body; on picking one of these upper lines out, we found that for the space necessary to cross the top of the design-unit, both its strands had been tinted before weaving in (weft-dyeing). These little colored lines or markers appeared, of course, on both sides of the fabric and must have made it quite easy for the weaver to paint identical patterns on each. They must also have been of great assistance in the original laying-out of the designs, for by introducing markers at regular intervals (ascertained by counting warps) along any single line of weft, regularity of spacing in a horizontal sense could be accomplished; by counting weft lines as they were woven upward from the one last marked and then marking a new weft, symmetrical vertical spacing could be insured (see plate 27, e; the shade of the markers is there exaggerated).

One further point: we experimented with water-color paints on bits of the bag fabric and found that it takes them without any blotting or running; furthermore the moisture in the paint (carrying very little of the color itself) quickly soaks through and shows on the reverse side in sharply defined wet areas of exactly the same shape as the painted figures. By painting over these moist areas the decorator was still further aided in the accuracy of the duplication of the design.

This painstaking reproduction was accomplished on nearly all the painted bags in the collection; there are but few specimens decorated on one side only. Its purpose is not obvious, for while the bags are reversible, the weave being the same within and without, specimens showing long use are much more worn on one side than on the other. It seems, therefore, that the patterns on the inside were normally invisible. That they were so meticulously carried out may be due to the strong craving for perfection and love for detail possessed by so many primitive craftsmen; or it may have resulted from an equally common psychological trait, namely that of wishing to carry over into a new technic the qualities of an older one. To be explicit: it is likely that basket-making was practised by these people before they learned to weave this specialized type of bag; the painted patterns under discussion are also found woven in the baskets (compare plate 24 with plates 26 and 28); hence it may be that when painting such decorations, it was thought proper that they should appear on both sides of the fabric as in baskets.

Fur cloth. This was one of the most important textile products of the Basket-makers. Robes of fur cloth were presumably the usual overgarment for cold weather, were doubtless used for sleeping blankets, and were invariably wrapped about the dead previous to burial; young babies were provided with specially shaped fur cloth coverings (plate 4, b, f).

The strings that compose the body of the fabric were variously prepared. The commonest method was to wrap a yucca cord with narrow strips of the hide of small animals applied raw and with the fur on; deer and mountain-sheep skins, when used, were generally dressed. The strips were applied spirally, the end of one piece holding down the beginning of the next. The tight wrapping of the hide caused the hair to stand out in all directions, thus giving the finished string the appearance of a greatly magnified pipe-cleaner. Another way of making the string was to catch tufts of long, woolly animal hair (dog or buffalo) detached from the hide,

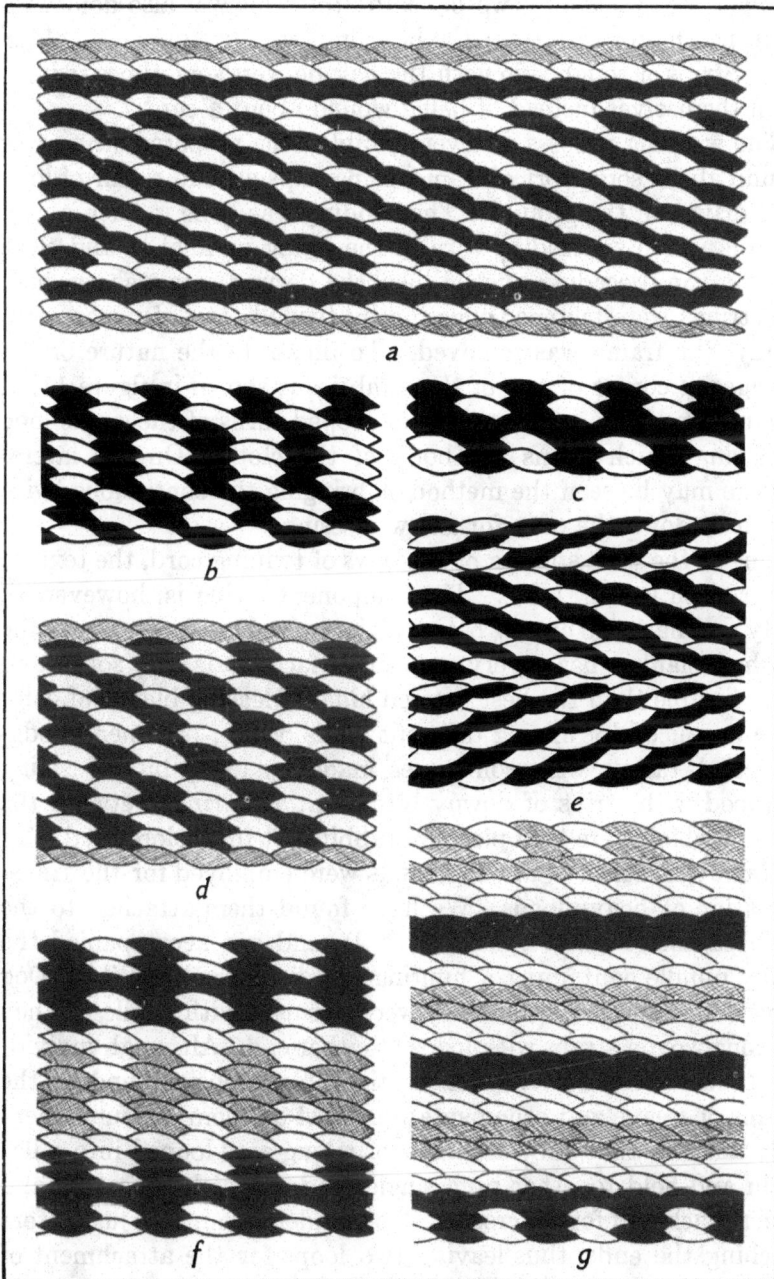

Twined weaving; designs produced by different manipulations of the weft-strands.

through the twists of a two-ply cord; the same was also done with small patches of skin from the heavily furred bottoms of rabbits' feet. Strips of tough skin with the hair on were sometimes twisted upon themselves instead of being wound about a cord.

The weaving process was very simple; the prepared string was wound about some sort of frame, or perhaps around a pair of long pegs driven in the ground. The winding was done in such a way as to lay each succeeding turn of the string parallel to and close against the preceding one. When the desired size was reached, the strings were fastened together by twined rows of yucca cord; finally, the frame was removed. To illustrate the nature of the selvages, a corner of one of these fabrics is shown in figure 11, a. The upper edge is composed of the looped turns of the single long fur-string which forms the body of the cloth. On the lateral selvage may be seen the method of bringing the continuous twining cords down the edge for a new crossing.

Due to the wide spacing of the rows of twining cord, the texture of fur cloth is very loose. The component string is, however, so fluffy and hangs so evenly between the twined cross-rows, that the finished blanket has a very smooth surface; it is also softer and more flexible than the best dressed hide. Pleasing blends of color were produced by mixing different kinds of fur; ornamental edgings and tassels were sometimes made by using bits of string wrapped with strips of downy bird skin; or strings between the plies of which were held pieces of rabbit foot fur, colored red.

Narrow Fabrics. Carrying bands were employed for the transportation of heavy loads. We have found them attached to the large pannier baskets (plate 23, k, l), and one accompanied the bulky bundle containing a hunting net discovered in White Dog Cave. It is probable that they were also used with cradles. They are long woven straps with loops at either end. Although individual specimens differ from each other in dimensions and in the details of weave and ornamentation, most of them are fundamentally alike in that they are made of a long cord looped into a flat skein and held together by a single binder, which runs over and under, back and forth across it. The binder terminates just before reaching the ends, thus leaving two loops for the attachment of the strap to the burden (see the diagrammatic drawing, plate 27, f). Ornamental patterns are sometimes introduced by making the skein of strings of contrasting colors, or by using a binder of a color different from the rest of the fabric.

One of the straps found with a pannier basket (plate 23, k) is made of a single heavy yucca fiber string looped on itself twelve times to form twenty-four parallel elements; the binder is also of yucca. The length of the specimen is 22 inches, width $1\frac{1}{2}$ inches. The second pannier strap is longer, 32 inches, but of the same width. It is composed of yellowish fiber and black human hair strings, alternated to produce a simple design; the binder is yucca. There are also several fragmentary bands of the same weave, in one of which (A–3495) the one remaining loop is tightly wound with fine string.

The band found with the rabbit net (plate 31, c) is constructed on the same basic principle, but its binder, instead of being covered by the longitudinal strings, forms the surface of the fabric. In making this strap, a single stout yucca cord was looped four times, producing eight parallel strings; the binder is woven back and forth over and under these; it is a heavy cord twisted of a mixture of dog and buffalo hair, and is so fluffy and is beaten up so tightly that the underlying yucca strings are entirely concealed except at the ends, where they protrude to form short loops for the attachment of tie-cords. The specimen is 22 inches long and $2\frac{1}{2}$ inches wide.

Tape. Very narrow flat fabrics were made on the same general principle as the coarser carrying-straps, but the materials are finer and the weave more elaborate. They are rare, our only new example being a short length of tape $\frac{5}{16}$ of an inch wide which was found attached, apparently as a tie-string, to a large fur cloth robe enveloping mummy 1, Cist 24, White Dog Cave. It has parallel longitudinal elements and a single binder; the parallel strings are twenty-eight in number, arranged in fourteen pairs which twine about the successive crossings of the binder instead of merely passing over and under them as in the carrying-straps. The design, produced by mixing brown and white strands, is very similar to that of a tape found in Cave 1, 1915. In number of elements and in weave the two specimens are identical.[1]

Rigid bands. We have only a single specimen of this type, but there is a very similar one from Grand Gulch in the American

---

[1] Kidder-Guernsey, 1919, p. 173 and figure 82.

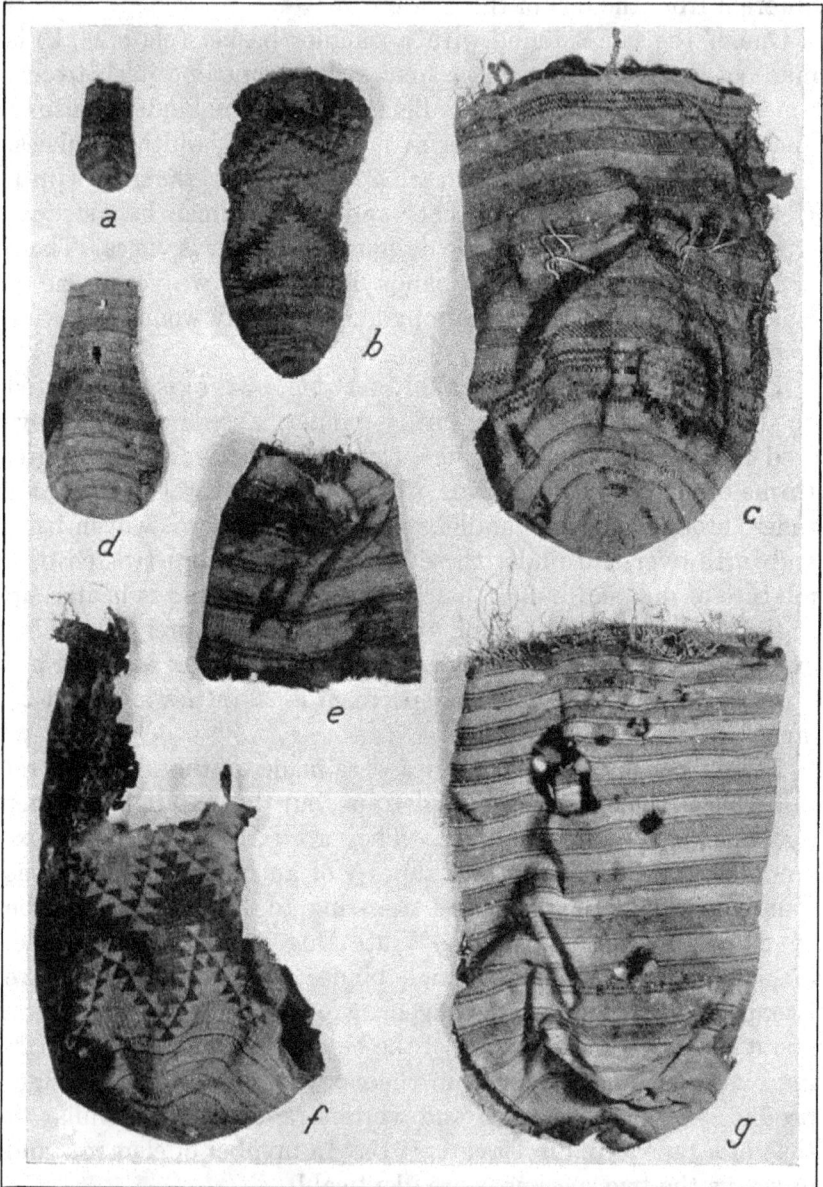

Twined-woven bags. All from White Dog Cave with the exception of d, which is from Cave 6. (About ⅓.)

Museum of Natural History in New York. Our example (White Dog Cave, A–3452) is composed of thirty slim, peeled willow twigs laid side by side to form a flat band 4½ inches wide and held together by a tight, twilled over-two-under-two weave of fine string. The upper part of the cross-weaving is in human hair string, the lower of apocynum. The object is 9½ inches long, but is broken off at both ends so that we cannot even guess at its original length, nor at the way in which it was finished.

NETTING AND CORDAGE

Coiled Netting.[1] A bag from White Dog Cave is our best example of this technic. It is a little apocynum string sack, 6 inches long, with rounded body and constricted neck. The stitch is very even and regular (plate 25, d); there are twelve coils to the inch and each coil has nine loops to the inch. The entire bottom of the bag is red; the neck is in natural color, encircled by narrow bands of red and brown. As there is no sign that new strings were introduced to make the changes in color, it seems probable that the entire fabric is made from a single long strand, which was stained or rubbed with pigment for the proper length whenever it was desired to produce a colored band.

Rabbit Net. This remarkable specimen, which, according to Dr. J. W. Fewkes, is probably the largest piece of ancient textile so far recovered in North America, is from White Dog Cave. When found it was rolled upon itself, partly wrapped in bunches of fiber, and tied into a neat bundle with yucca leaves. Undone and spread out, it proved to be a net 240 feet long, 3 feet 8 inches wide, and with meshes 2½ inches square. It is in perfect condition and, except for a single strand which has at some time been burned through by a stray spark, is as firm and strong as the day it was made. The material is a two-ply twine of Indian hemp (*Apocynum cannabinum*), very firm and evenly twisted and about $\frac{3}{32}$ of an inch in diameter. An estimate of the amount of string composing the net gives approximately 19,581 feet, or very nearly 3¾ miles. Extending the length of the long edges and across the ends is a marginal cord, of stouter two-ply yucca string; the method of attaching this can be seen in plate 31. The mesh-knot is one that is

[1] This term has been suggested by Mr. Willoughby as a more appropriate one than Mason's "coil without foundation"; for a diagram of the weave, see Kidder-Guernsey, 1919, figure 45.

used almost universally. The entire net is of the same mesh, but there are two sections, one 9 and the other 6 feet long, in which human hair has been used with the apocynum fiber, one strand of hair twisted with one of fiber.[1] These sections are naturally of a darker color than the rest of the specimen. Strung on the cord of one of the meshes is a single olivella shell bead, another bears two stone beads; still another has attached to it a few downy feathers which may be seen in the plate; on a fourth is a small pink feather, and at a fifth place there is a paw of some small animal tied on with sinew.

Attached to the net when found was a carrying-strap of coarse dog or buffalo fur-string. Such a strap was no doubt needed for transporting the net, as the whole bundle weighs over twenty-eight pounds. The bunches of fiber that partly enclosed the rolled up net are of Indian hemp (the same material in its raw state as the twine); it is stripped up and tied in hanks in much the same manner as are the trade bundles of Indian hemp in the Peabody Museum collected from the Thompson Indians.

The method of using nets such as this is made clear by the following quotation from Powell:[2]

They (the Paiute) get many rabbits sometimes with arrows sometimes with nets. They make a net of twine, made of the fibers of a native flax. Sometimes this is made a hundred yards in length, and is placed in a half-circular position, with wings of sage brush. They have a circle hunt, and drive great numbers of rabbits into the snare, where they are shot with arrows.

It has occurred to us that the hair string sections, being darker than the rest, might have been intended to lure the quarry toward them, for, to a frightened animal they might appear to be openings.

Of interest because of its close similarity to the present specimen is a rabbit net in the Peabody Museum that was collected from the Paiutes about 1870 by Dr. Edward Palmer. Its length is 124 feet, width 4 feet. The mesh is practically the same, and the material is also apocynum fiber; furthermore, there are sections which appear darker than the rest of the body, though no human hair string is used. This net is provided with a number of light crotched sticks which were used to hold it upright when set. No such sticks were

---

[1] From Cave 10 came a fragment of another net of the same weave and mesh size; this piece is also made of human hair and apocynum string.

[2] 1875, p. 127.

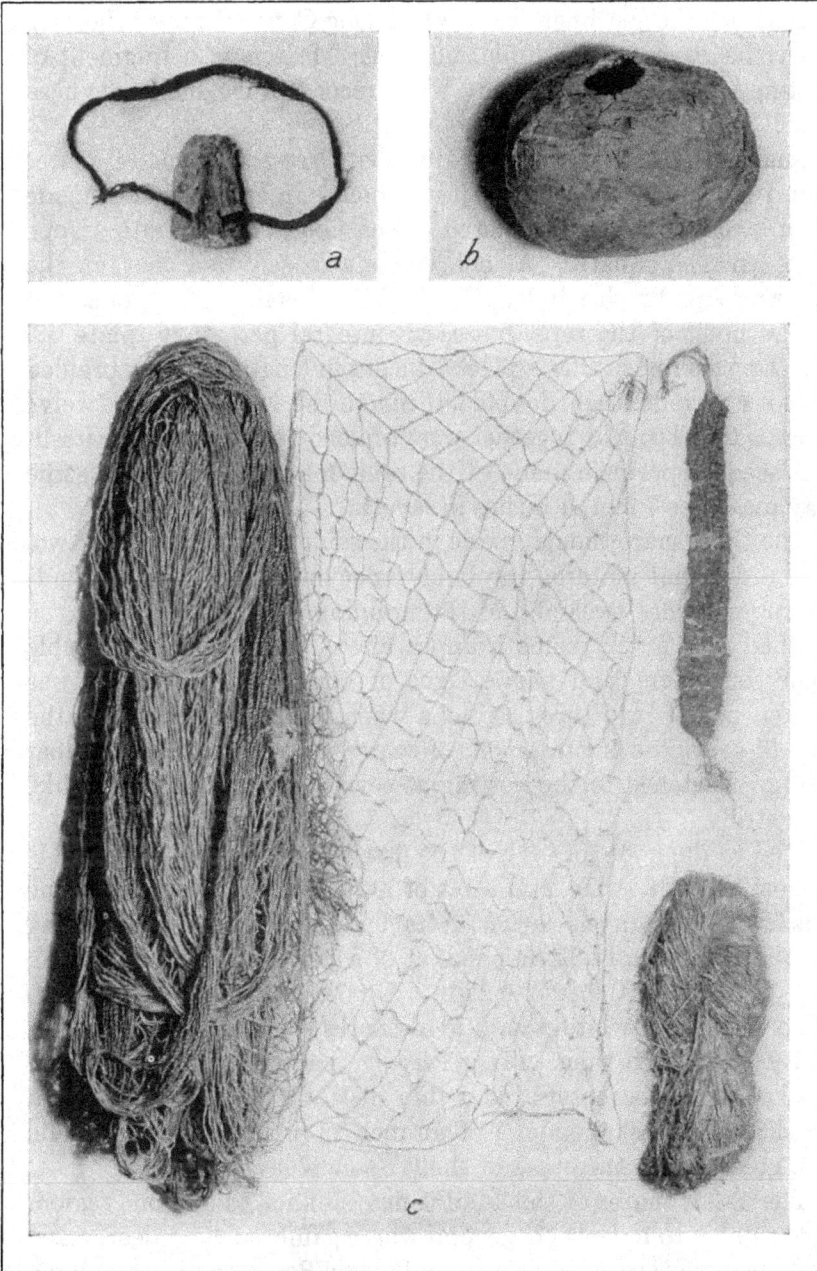

WHITE DOG CAVE

a, Umbilical pad; b, Gourd vessel; c, Rabbit-net, carrying-strap and bunch of fiber
found with the net. (About 1/10.)

found with the specimen from White Dog Cave. In the collection from the caves of Coahuila, northern Mexico, is a fragment of netting similar to the above. Heye records a fragment of yucca rabbit net from a Diegueño cache pot.[1]

Snares. The best preserved of the three specimens of snares found in Cave 6, measures 8 feet 6 inches in length and is made from twelve strands of twisted yucca fiber, braided into a rope $\frac{5}{16}$ of an inch square. At one end is a loosely tied knot, at the other a loop, 2 inches in length. This loop is not spliced or seized to the body of the rope, but is an integral part of it (plate 32, a). To accomplish this, a piece 7 inches in length was first braided with six strands, then doubled to make the loop, and the twelve strands thus brought together were braided to form the rope itself.

A second specimen made of the same material and in the same way measures 7 feet, 4 inches in length.

The third snare though made in the same way as the other two, is of a different material, probably apocynum fiber. The strands are more evenly twisted and the braiding so done as to give the finished rope a very smooth appearance. It is also more flexible than the others, and shows signs of considerable use. It was broken or cut into three sections when found. Attached to the loop of the noose is a fragment of coarse netting made of soft fiber string. Fastened to the netting at several points is a thread-like fiber string.

Tied to the noose of each of the first two specimens described is a short piece of twine, and a bit of netting made of similar twine was found loose in the cache. Attached to one end of this netting are four beads and a little pendant of a material resembling opal, very brilliant in the proper light. Of the beads, the one next to the pendant is of white stone and measures $\frac{1}{8}$ of an inch in diameter, and $\frac{1}{16}$ of an inch thick. It is very symmetrical. Another white bead of the same material is a thin disk. The third and fourth are discoidal in shape and $\frac{1}{4}$ of an inch in diameter; one is made of a green stone, the other of shell, *Spondylus calcifer*.

The use of snares of this kind is not confined to any one region, but appears to have been general where game, such as deer, antelope, or mountain-sheep, was found. The Pomo Indians employ a similar contrivance, the noose, when set, filled with coarse netting.

[1] 1919, p. 45.

Lumholtz describes and figures a snare used by the Huichol Indians of central Mexico, which is set with a netting across the noose opening.[1] Waterman illustrates a Yahi deer snare of the same type as those under discussion, but without the netting.[2] It is probable that the Cliff-dwellers also used snares, as one of a series of pictographs found near Ruin 5 by the 1914 expedition depicts a man in the act of throwing a noose over the head of a mountain-sheep.[3]

The netting with which the noose was filled no doubt made the trap more effective, as it could be set to cover a much wider space in the runway. The animal in pushing its way through the net would draw the noose tight about its neck.

The method of braiding a rope square is also widespread and has survived into modern times as in Navajo leather riatos. Examples are found principally in regions where the lariat is used, though the Northwest Coast tribes braid ropes in this way for their harpoons and other fishing devices, as do the Mohave for neck strings.

A running noose probably designed for a snare is the clever little device illustrated in plate 32, b. The braided loop is replaced by a short section of hollow bone, neatly cut and seized to one end of the string with sinew. This makes a very free-running noose.

OBJECTS OF WOOD

Atlatl or Spear-thrower. The atlatl is a device which serves to add greater length, and therefore, greater propulsive force to the arm of the thrower in launching a spear or dart. It consists of a long, thin stick with a grip for the hand at one end, and a hook-like spur to engage the butt of the spear at the other. In throwing, the butt of the spear was placed against the spur at the end of the atlatl; its shaft lay flat along the atlatl with its point project-ing in front of the user's hand; it was held in this position, prob-ably near its middle, by the second (fore) and third fingers which passed through the loops of the atlatl on the sides of the grip. The fourth and fifth fingers were clenched upon the atlatl grip below the loops, holding it firmly against the palm and heel of the hand. The base of the thumb served to solidify this grip on the atlatl,

[1] Lumholtz, 1903, Vol. II, p. 41.
[2] Waterman, 1918, plate 13.
[3] Kidder-Guernsey, 1919, plate 93, b.

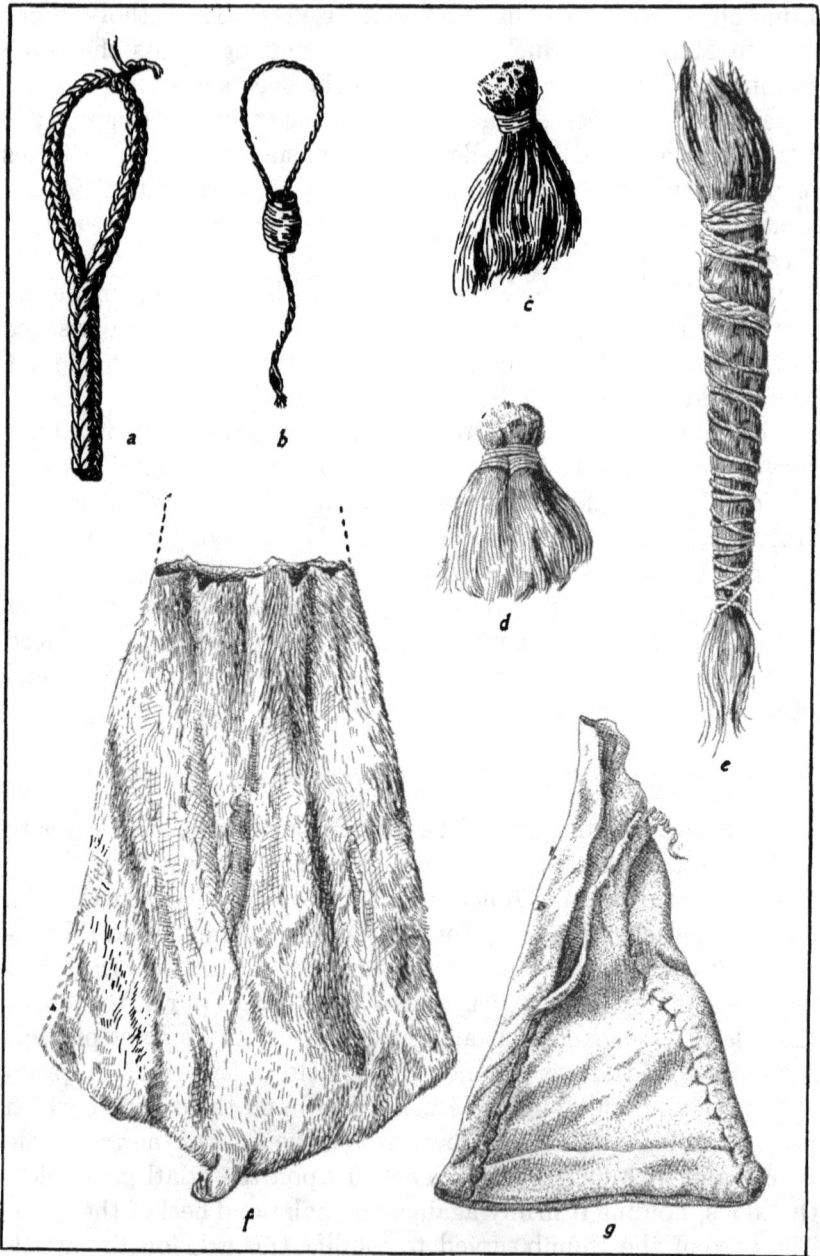

a, b, Snares showing details; c, d, e, Bunches of human hair; f, g, Skin bags.
b, c, d, f, g, White Dog Cave; a, Cave 6; e, Cave 14. (About ½.)

and the thumb proper aided to steady the spear in its resting place between and upon the second and third fingers.[1]

The atlatls illustrated in the plate were all found with burials in White Dog Cave. The finest of these, plate 33, b, c, had been broken nearly in two before it was placed in the cist. It is made of oak, carefully worked down and almost polished. The length over all is 25 inches. The front or spur side is nearly flat, except for the short distance between the spur and the distal end, where the middle is a little higher than the rest of the surface. The sides are rounded and the back is slightly convex. The distal end terminates in a blunt point. The spur is set at the head of a short deep groove, the bottom and sides of which show plainly the marks of the sharp stone tool used in excavating it. At $3\frac{1}{2}$ inches from the rounded proximal or hand end the two sides of the stick have broad notches; these notches lie between the finger-loops. The latter are made of a single strip of heavy dressed hide folded lengthwise. Through the middle of this folded piece there is cut a longitudinal slit just large enough to allow it to be pushed up over the atlatl shaft to its proper position at the lower end of the side grooves. The two flaps are brought forward and down until they touch the stick at the upper end of these grooves, where they are securely fastened with strong sinew sewed through them, and then wrapped around the shaft. On the back of the atlatl there is a thong which is looped through the slit in the grip, brought forward and seized to the shaft; this served to hold the strip in place and to keep the finger loops properly extended.

Tightly lashed to the back of the atlatl, as shown in the drawing, are three beautifully worked greenish stones of elongated loaf-shape, flat where they lie against the wood, their upper sides sharply convex. All three are fashioned from a substance identified by Professor J. B. Woodworth as a fossilized mammalian tooth.[2] The entire shaft, from the binding which holds the upper stone to the finger-loop attachments, is coated with a thin layer of resinous gum, applied before the stones were tied on, but afterwards renewed on the front side, where it covers the seizing of the middle one.

[1] See Kidder-Guernsey, 1919, figure 87.

[2] An unworked fragment of the same material was found in a bag in Cave 6; see plate 44, b.

The second atlatl (plate 33, f) is somewhat less well-preserved, its oak shaft being checked and a little shrunken, and the finger-loops dried stiff. The lateral curve of the stick is probably due to warping. The total length is 23½ inches. The spur is slimmer and sharper than that of the specimen just described; and the groove, instead of being deep and short, is shallow and runs nearly 5 inches down the shaft. The finger-loops are straddled as before, over a pair of broad notches in the side of the stick; they are made by folding a buckskin strip, slitting it in the middle, and drawing it over the shaft, to which the ends are attached by a cross-binding and an over-wrapping of sinew. The slit middle part is kept from slipping backward by an annular seizing. Ten inches from the butt there may be seen on the front (illustrated) side of the weapon the print of a former ligature; on the back there is a light colored oval mark corresponding exactly in size and shape to the flat base of a chipped stone (plate 35, f) found loose in the same cist. These traces indicate, of course, that the stone was once attached to the back of the weapon.

The next atlatl to be considered is a fragmentary one, shown in plate 33, d. The part recovered is a section of the shaft 7¾ inches long extending forward from the former seat of the finger-loops. To the back is attached an elaborate series of "weights." The specimen was found, done up with other objects, in a skin container that was tucked between the outer coverings and the fur cloth robe of mummy 2, Cist 24. Both ends are bruised and rounded, indicating that the piece was used in some way, perhaps as a ceremonial object or as a fetish, for a long time after the original weapon was broken.

In size and shape the fragment differs little from corresponding parts of the atlatls described above. The side grooves under the missing finger-loops are shallower; and there are a pair of notches just forward of these, which once held the fastenings of the front ends of the loops. Of the attached "weights," the lowest is a small triangular chipped point, 1⅜ inches long and ⅝ of an inch wide; its lower side is flat, so that it fits snugly against the stick, the upper side is somewhat rounded. The sinew wrappings which hold it pass about the shallow finger notches. Two and three-quarters inches above the chipped point there is a flat oval piece of white limestone, 1⅜ inches long, ½ inch wide, and ⅛ of an inch thick;

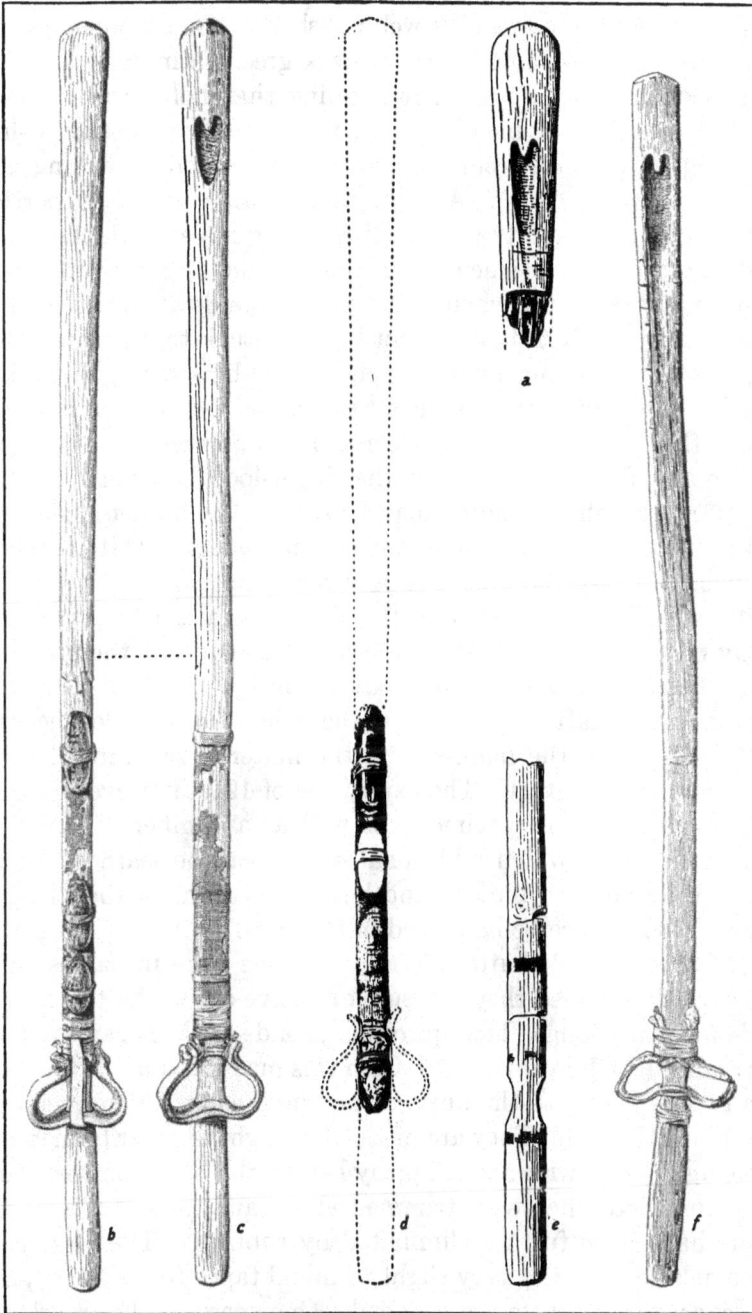

WHITE DOG CAVE
Atlatls or dart-throwers. (About ¼.)

it is very neatly made and is well polished. Almost touching this is a polished, loaf-shaped piece of dark green satin spar, 2 inches long. Pushed under the sinew binding that holds the latter in place is a section, 1 inch long, broken from a round skewer-like bone object, perhaps from a pin such as was used in making hair ornaments (plate 18, b). A dark, pitchy stain covers that portion of the shaft to which the objects just described are attached, and is smeared over the sinew wrappings of the two forward ones. Adhering to the stick when found were some downy feathers, but it is not certain that they had not become stuck to it accidentally.

The two remaining figures of the plate show pieces of broken atlatls. The butt fragment has two narrow notches on one side below the finger-grooves, a feature not observed in any other specimen. Ligature prints of the finger-loop attachments, and also of a " weight " binding may be seen. The broken distal end is the heaviest and broadest one in the collection; it measures $1\frac{3}{8}$ inches across; the groove is $2\frac{3}{4}$ inches long.

Darts. The darts cast with the aid of the atlatl consisted normally of two parts: a long main-shaft, feathered at the proximal or butt end; and a short foreshaft set into the tip or distal end of the main-shaft. Heretofore there has been little accurate knowledge as to the main-shafts, the material recovered having been very fragmentary. The expedition of 1916, however, yielded three nearly perfect specimens, as well as a number of less complete ones, from which additional details can be learned. These were all found with burials, and had, on account of their length, been broken before being placed in the cists.

The three entire shafts referred to above were in halves when discovered; mended they measure exclusive of foreshafts, $52\frac{1}{2}$, 55, and $55\frac{1}{2}$ inches long. The tips or distal ends are the heaviest parts averaging $\frac{1}{2}$ inch in thickness; from this maximum diameter there is a gradual taper to the butts or proximal ends, which average $\frac{3}{8}$ of an inch through. They are made of straight, slender branches of some light wood with a small pithy heart; the bark has been carefully removed, the twigs trimmed close, and in some cases the knots have been further eliminated by rubbing. The large ends of some shafts have a very slight terminal taper (plate 34, h), and the edges of the butts are rounded. One specimen has marks on its surface such as might have been caused by using a shaft-straightener of the wrench type.[1]

In the distal or large end of the shaft is drilled a cone-shaped hole $\frac{5}{16}$ of an inch in diameter at the mouth and 1 inch to $1\frac{1}{4}$ inches in depth; into this socket was fitted the butt of the foreshaft as in j. In order to prevent the socket from being split open when the fore-shaft was driven back into it on impact, it is reënforced by outer ferrule-like wrappings of stout flat sinew as shown in the drawing. The proximal or butt end of the main-shaft is provided with a shallow cup, b, to engage the spur of the throwing stick, and here again there is sometimes applied a band of sinew to prevent splitting.

The method of winging the shafts can be accurately reconstructed from the material at hand. As shown in a, b, three feathers possibly somewhat trimmed, but with unsplit quills, were laid along the shaft and seized to it at both ends with flat sinew.[2] The average length of the feathers on five specimens is $7\frac{1}{2}$ inches; the average distance from the end of the feathering to the butt is $4\frac{1}{2}$ inches. The feathers themselves were prepared for attachment as follows: the end of the quill was cut off and into its hollow body there was introduced a tight fitting plug, 1 inch to $1\frac{1}{2}$ inches long, either of wood or of the sharp, hard tip of a yucca leaf. The end of the quill was further solidified by wrapping it about with sinew. Both these features are illustrated in b.[3] Heavy flat seizing of sinew secures the thus prepared lower end of the feather to the shaft; the light tip end has no extra strengthening and is merely bound to the shaft with a few turns of thin sinew. The purpose of this careful plugging and binding of the quill was undoubtedly to render it so firm and solid that it could be tightly bound to the shaft at exactly the correct angle; an unplugged quill would have been crushed by the ligatures, and the feather

[1] Though not uncommon in cliff-dwellings, we have found no such implement among Basket-maker remains. The Cliff-dweller wrenches are made of mountain-sheep horn, are 9 to 10 inches long, and have a hole, or a series of holes of different sizes, in one end; through these the shaft was drawn and then straightened by leverage on the other end (see Kidder-Guernsey, 1919, plate 46, a, e). See also Hough, 1919, plate 46, figure 4.

[2] We are now able to rectify an error in our previous report. In our restoration of the feathering of atlatl darts there given (figure 89) we were misled by the presence of some extra seizing bands not really connected with the feathering, and postulated a triple attachment like that on lower Yukon shafts. This is incorrect.

[3] Although we have not seen the specimens, we think it likely that the loose ends of cords bound under the seizing of the feathers on darts described by Pepper (1905, p. 121) represent the remains of feather-butt reinforcements similar to those just described.

117

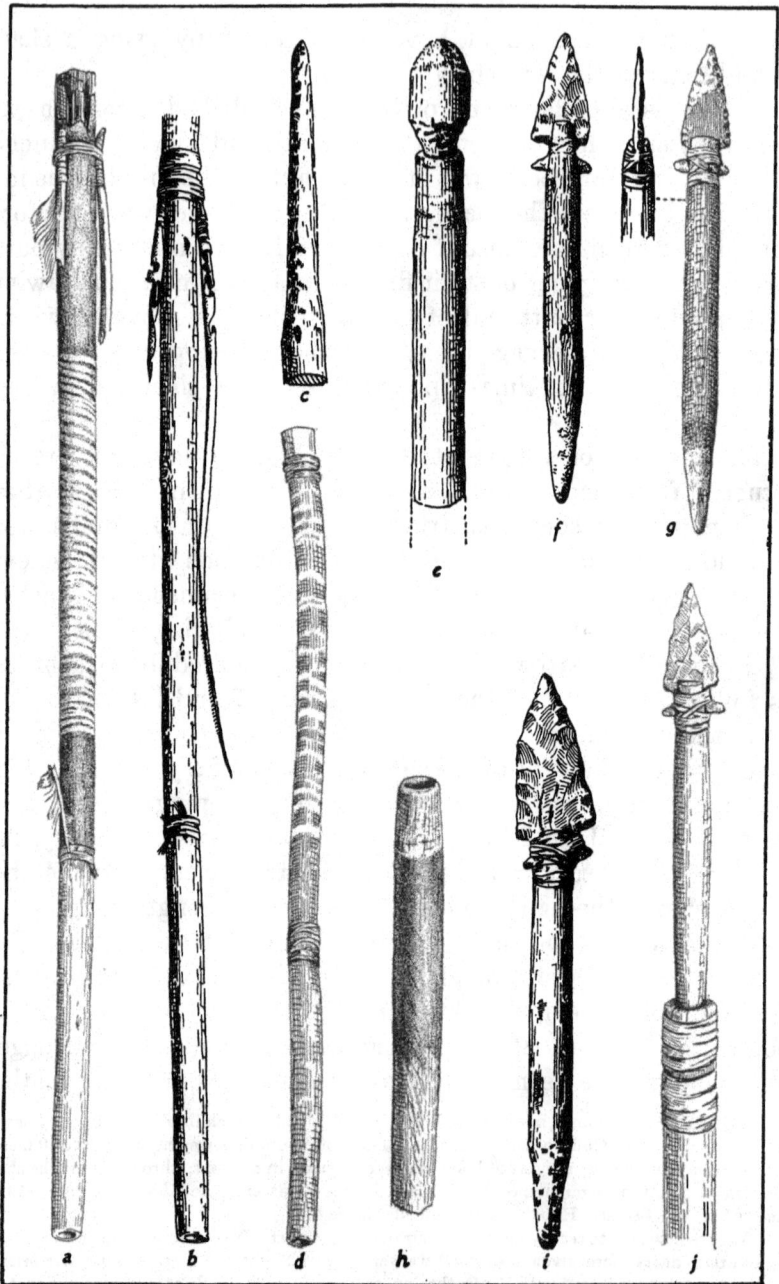

WHITE DOG CAVE

a, b, d, Lower portion of darts showing method of feathering; c, Point of dart; e, Upper
portion of dart showing bunt-head; h, Upper portion of shaft showing socket for foreshaft;
f, g, i, Foreshafts with chipped stone points; j, Foreshaft in position, and upper portion of
shaft.   (About ¼.)

would not have held rigidly to its intended position. The arrangement just described is, as far as we know, unique in shaft feathering, but is found in the feather hair ornaments of the Mohave (P. M. catalogue number 10091).

So little of the pile of the feathers has resisted decay and the ravages of insects that it is impossible to identify the species of birds from which they were obtained. Plumes of corresponding length and weight, tied into bundles and perhaps intended for the winging of darts, were found in Cave 1, Kinboko, in 1915 (Kidder-Guernsey 1919, plate 81; a, b); these belonged to Hutchin's (?) wild goose (*Branta canadensis hutchinsi*) and the western red-tailed hawk (*Buteo borealis calurus*).

A non-functional feature of the main-shafts remains to be described, namely, decoration. All the darts are painted or stained on the shaftment under the feathering, and also for a short distance back from the socket end; some, we judge from fragments, were colored their entire length. The most elaborately decorated shaftment (plate 34, a) is painted black with a spiral line of red; a second (d) was painted black over a temporary wrapping, which when removed left a spiral ornament in the light natural color of the wood. Another, on which the paint shows but faintly, seems to bear four broad longitudinal lines separated from each other by narrow stripes of natural surface. Most of the socket ends were painted black as shown in h, two, however, are red; and one socket end 25 inches long is stained black for 15 inches, thence to the break it is light red.

In the collection are a few broken main-shafts that have been put to secondary uses. The flint-flaker shown in figure 15, b, c, is mounted on such a fragment; another piece, from the butt-end of a dart, was whittled to a sharp point and served as a skewer-like pin for fastening together the wrappings of a mummy.

Foreshafts, complete with points, are represented by five perfect specimens from White Dog Cave. All of these are tapered at one end to fit into the socket of the spear shaft, and are notched at the other to provide a seat for the stone tip. The one shown in i, plate 34, formed part of a bundle resting in the lap of a mummy in Cist 31; it is the largest in the collection.[1] It is made from a peeled stick unworked except at the ends. The point is of red

[1] See table of measurements at end of description.

119

jasper and is secured to the stick by a seizing of heavy sinew. The one illustrated in f, found near the right hand of mummy 2, Cist 27, is slightly tapered at the notched end. The red jasper point is firmly wedged in the notch; the sinew bindings were in place when the specimen was found, but crumbled away on exposure to the air. Specimens g, and j, lay at the foot of mummy 1, Cist 24. The latter is flattened on either side at the notched end; its head is of yellow jasper and is secured to the shaft by a neat seizing of fine flat sinew applied very tightly. The body of the shaft is painted with a thin grey wash; at the notched end on either side are daubs of thick dark red paint put on over the wrappings and also discoloring the base of the chipped point. The head of g, is worked from a thin spall of dark flint, the original surface of the flake showing on one side. It is fastened to the shaft with flat sinew. The shaft itself is colored with dark red paint which ends where the taper begins, showing that it was tinted after it had been inserted in the main-shaft of the dart.

MEASUREMENTS OF FORESHAFTS IN INCHES

	A	B	C	D
Total length	$6\frac{3}{4}$	$5\frac{5}{8}$	6	$5\frac{3}{8}$
Length of shaft	$4\frac{3}{4}$	$4\frac{1}{2}$	$4\frac{3}{4}$	$4\frac{1}{8}$
Diameter of shaft	$\frac{1}{2}$	$\frac{7}{16}$	$\frac{3}{8}$	$\frac{3}{8}$
Length of head	$2\frac{1}{4}$	$1\frac{3}{4}$	$1\frac{5}{8}$	$1\frac{1}{2}$
Width of head at base	1	$\frac{3}{4}$	$\frac{5}{8}$	$\frac{3}{4}$

Comparing these with the dimensions of foreshafts from southeastern Utah given by Pepper (1905, p. 127), it will be seen that the latter average considerably larger.

On plate 34, e, is shown a wooden bunt head tightly wedged into the socket of the main-shaft, beyond the end of which it protrudes for $1\frac{1}{2}$ inches. The rounded end is $\frac{3}{4}$ of an inch in diameter. It is roughly finished and is much like a specimen figured in our first report, which we thought might possibly be a bunt head for an atlatl dart.[1]

Pepper,[2] illustrates several foreshafts with bunt heads of bone fitted down over them. Nothing of this sort is in the collection, but there is a main-shaft, c, whose distal end, instead of being provided with the usual socket, is brought to a plain tapering point.

[1] Kidder-Guernsey, 1919, figure 92 and p. 185.

[2] 1905, plate III.

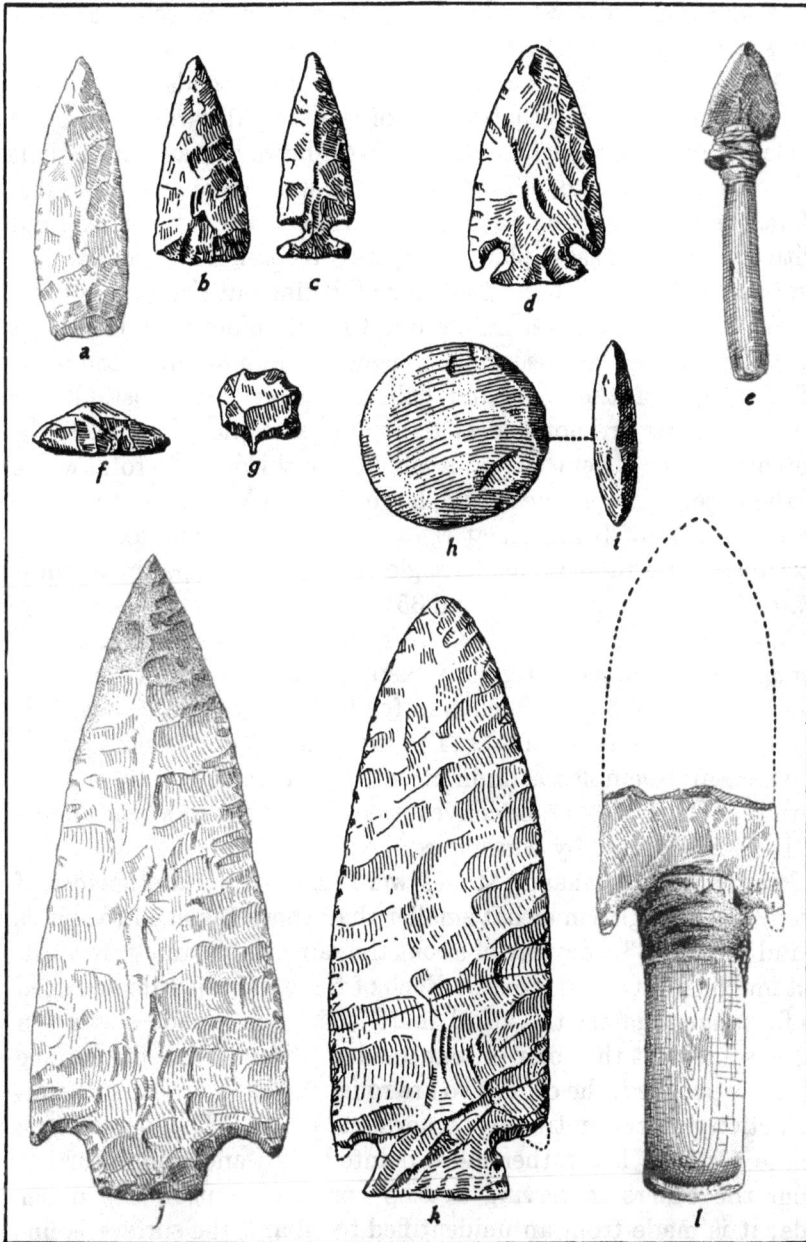

a, b, Unfinished foreshaft points; c, Foreshaft point; d, Chipped knife blade; e, Hafted pipe-drill; f, Chipped atlatl stone; g, Chipped flint graver; h, i, Unfinished flint disc; j, k, Chipped knife blades; l, Flint knife (blade broken). a, f, h, i, j, k, l, White Dog Cave; b, c, d, g, Burial cave, Sayodneechee Canyon; e, Cave 6. (About ⅓.)

It is possible that a bone head was slipped on over this, and the foreshaft dispensed with.

Dart Points.[1] All the chipped atlatl dart heads which were found attached to foreshafts were of the tanged variety. From a skeleton in Sayodneechee Cave (1914), however, and in a little skin sack from Cist 6, White Dog Cave, were recovered a number of points similar in size and shape to the tanged specimens but with unnotched bases (plate 35, a, b). We believe these are dart heads completed up to the final step of flaking out the deep notches on the lower sides, a step deferred until just before mounting them in the foreshafts, because of the danger in an unmounted condition of breakage of the long and delicate flanges. Almost all our finished points are notched at right angles to their long axes, the notches having a depth equal to about one-third of the total width of the base. The notches of the large chipped knives, on the other hand, instead of being set at right angles to the long axes of the specimens, run in at an acute angle (compare the specimens illustrated in the two plates, 34 and 35).

Atlatl Stones. On plate 35, f, is illustrated a chipped object thought to have been originally fastened to the back of the atlatl shown in f, plate 33, which was found in the same cist with it (Cist 24, White Dog Cave). The material is translucent quartz; in shape it resembles a diminutive " turtle-back " with one flat surface. On the upper, or convex, side are faint marks that appear to have been made by wrappings.

Four small loaf-shaped stones were taken from the bottom of Cist 27. Though somewhat smaller than those fastened to atlatls b and d, plate 33, they are of about the same shape and were without much doubt atlatl stones. Each of them has one side flattened to fit snugly against the atlatl shaft. Three are made of a green stone somewhat the color of, but less hard than, jade; the surface of one is polished, the other two are roughened as if by some chemical action, but retain traces of an original polish. The fourth stone (plate 17, f, g) has rather more pointed ends and differs further from the others in having a deep concavity cut in the under side; it is made from an unidentified fossil and the surface is unpolished.

---

[1] These and the following specimens (atlatl stones) are treated here, rather than under their proper place among the stone objects, because they are really integral parts of the atlatl.

Another specimen is perhaps an unfinished atlatl stone; parts of its surface show chipping, others grinding. The material is the same as in the group of three described above.

Grooved Clubs. On plate 36, f, g, are shown two of these objects. The collection contains four complete specimens and one fragment. The former are from burial cists in White Dog Cave, and the fragment is from a looted and partly burned-out burial cist in Cave 6. The best preserved of these is one of a pair found with the mummy of an adult male in Cist 27. It is 20½ inches in length, 2 inches wide at the broad end, and tapers to 1½ inches in width at the small end; the average thickness is ⅝ of an inch. The warping of the stick may be partly accidental as it will be noted that the two specimens figured are not bent in the same direction. The edges and broad surfaces are rounded (see cross-section of the one illustrated in g). On each side are four deep parallel longitudinal grooves 17 inches long, with a break at one point as shown in the drawing. These grooves are neatly made, evenly spaced, V-shaped cuts. Two inches from the small end the club is ringed by a deep groove, set at a slight angle and widened at one edge to a broad curved notch; in the groove are traces of cord or sinew wrapping. A cement-like substance, thickest about the edge of the notch, still adheres to one side of the stick, and seems to have been put on over the wrappings. It is possible that the groove and notch may represent a seat for a wrist cord. There are two other much shallower encircling grooves, one 4 inches, the other 5¼ inches from the small end; in these also are marks of wrappings. All surfaces of the club show careful finish, but no traces of paint, the only color being a thin red line in one of the grooves which is probably a print from a wrapping cord. The edges and ends of the stick are not bruised or battered. Because of age and partial decay the club now weighs but 2½ ounces, but an undecayed fragment from Cave 6 shows the original wood to have been dense and heavy.

The foregoing description will answer for all the clubs in the collection, as they show little individual variation. While we can assign no specific use to these objects, we do not think they are rabbit-sticks such as those used among the Pueblo tribes.[1] Most of the latter differ from these in some details, particularly the

[1] Mr. C. C. Willoughby has suggested that they may have been used to ward off spears after the manner in which the natives of one of the Solomon Islands use an odd-shaped club for fending off spears, and also as a weapon of defense.

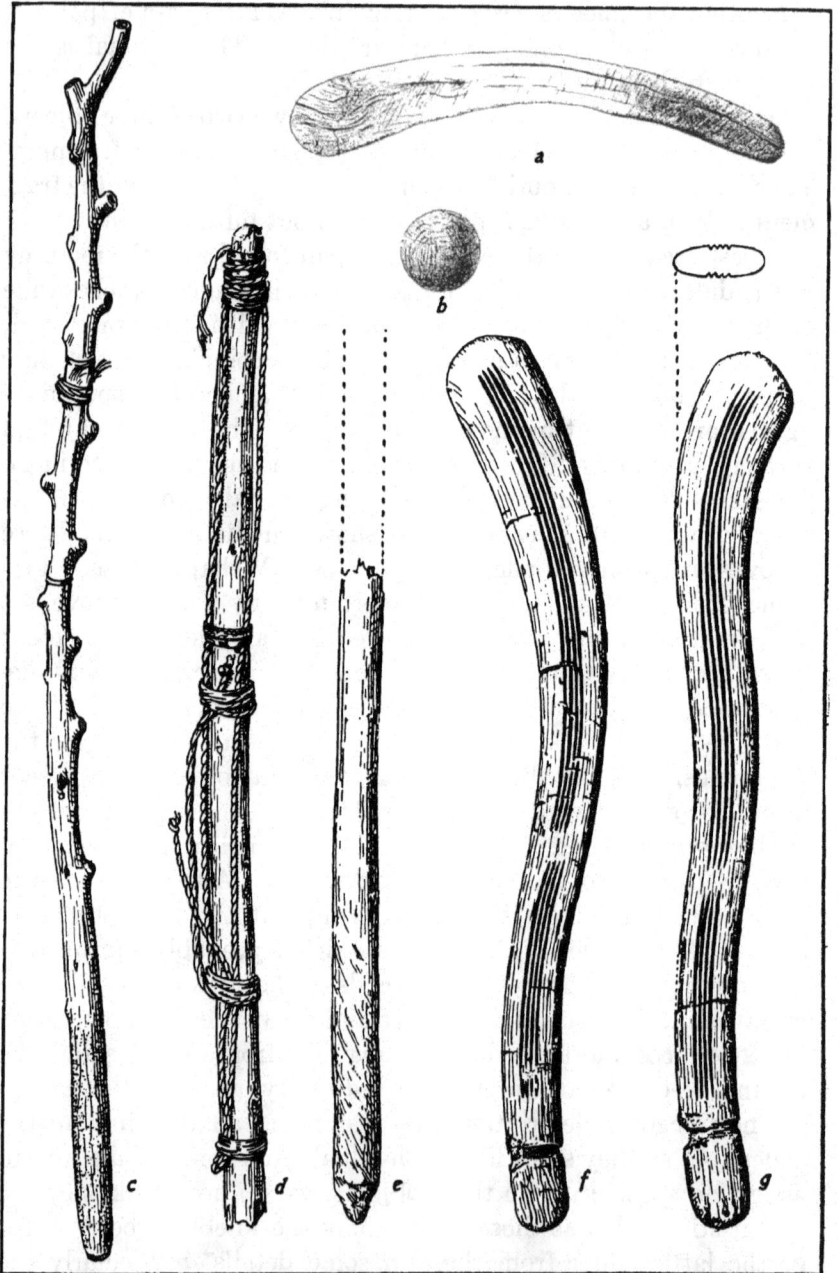

a, Wooden implement; b, Wooden gaming ball; c, Ceremonial stick; d, e, Opposite ends
of wooden device; f, g, Grooved clubs accompanying atlatls. All from White Dog Cave
except a, which is from Cave 14. (b, about ½; a, c–g, about 1/5.)

familiar type used by the Hopi, which in addition to having a hand grip cut at one end, is as a rule decorated by a painting with a pre-scribed design, one element of which is a pair of black markings symbolizing rabbit ears or rabbit feet. An ungrooved rabbit-stick, 6 inches longer than our grooved clubs but somewhat resembling them in shape, is in the Peabody Museum. It was collected by Dr. Edward Palmer in 1875 from the Diegueño Indians and is cata-logued as a "boomerang." Clubs identical with our specimens were found in a pit-shrine near Laguna, New Mexico, by Mrs. Parsons,[1] and Hough figures one from a cave near Lava, New Mexico.[2] In the Peabody Museum are fragments of two grooved clubs from Yucatan which differ from ours only in that the broad surfaces and the edges are flat instead of rounded, and that there are a greater number of the parallel grooves. The sculptures of Chichen Itza frequently depict these clubs, usually in the hands of warriors who also carry atlatls and atlatl spears. One is figured most real-istically on the sculptured top of an altar in the outer chamber or vestibule of the Temple of the Tigers, where it is shown in the left hand of a warrior, who bears as well an atlatl and sheaf of spears.

In company with all the grooved clubs noted either atlatls or some adjunct of the atlatl were found. The significance of this is two-fold; first, that it aids in establishing the identity of the Laguna pit-shrine and Lava cave specimens as Basket-maker; second, that it shows these clubs to be a distinct type used by a people who also used the atlatl. That the Laguna clubs were found with other offerings most of which were feather sticks of relatively recent make does not, to our minds, affect the question of their antiquity; the probable explanation of their presence in the shrine being that they were found in a Basket-maker cave by some Pueblo Indian who regarded them as appropriate offerings for the same reason that ancient arrow points are still prized by the Pueblos as fetishes. This seems all the more likely as the Zuñi are said by Mr. Cushing to have recovered baskets from prehistoric deposits.[3]

Planting Sticks. In plate 37 is a series of planting sticks: num-bers a, c, d, and g were found in Cist 24, White Dog Cave; e and f are from Cave 9.

The one shown in g, we regard as a type specimen of Basket-maker planting stick; it is 45 inches in length and is made from a

---

[1] Parsons, 1918, figures 36, 38, 39.   [2] Hough, 1914, p. 19, figure 21.   [3] Ibid., 1919, p. 267.

root of some hardwood tree, possibly oak. The whole surface has been smoothed by grinding, but very little altered in shape. The smoothing process has removed all bark except that in the deep depressions such as occur in roots. One end has been worked down to a thin blade having a rounded point and one sharp edge. The blade is 2 inches in width and begins 17 inches from the end of the stick. It has a smooth, almost polished surface. The crook at the proximal end is natural, but it gives the implement a nice balance when held in position for use. This specimen shows long service.

The sticks represented in e, f, differ but little from the one just described. Both are made from roots; f, is 42½ inches in length and has a very thin blade with one sharp edge; e, is 32 inches in length with a blade 2⅜ inches wide, sharp on the end and curved edge.

The Cliff-dweller planting sticks which correspond to these in form are much lighter in weight with thinner blades, and nearly straight, carefully shaped handles that normally terminate in round knobs.[1]

The one figured in a, found with mummy 1 in Cist 24, is of a different type, having a plain flattened point instead of a thin-edged blade; it is 49 inches in length and averages ⅞ of an inch in diameter. One end is worked down to a flat point, the other end has an artificial crook. It is made from a peeled limb of some hard wood. Knots are rubbed down and smoothed. This stick is dark in color and polished for its entire length by handling and wear.

The specimen shown in b, from Cist 6, White Dog Cave, is made from a heavy greasewood stick; it has a flattened point like the one just described. Simple sticks of this nature are also common in cliff-dwellings, and are used today by the Navajo.

The implement, c, is made from a rather light wood and has a neatly tapered point; the crook at the small end is partly natural; d is 32 inches long and is made of a slender greasewood stick; it has a long finely tapering point. The entire length of the implement has been smoothed and rounded. The point is slightly polished.

Scoop-like Objects. Wooden objects similar to those represented on plate 38, g, h, i, were found so regularly in Basket-maker

---

[1] See Kidder-Guernsey, 1919, plate 47, d, e; the stick shown in plate 47, c, we now think is probably Basket-maker. It was found with a disturbed burial in a small cave in Sagi Canyon.

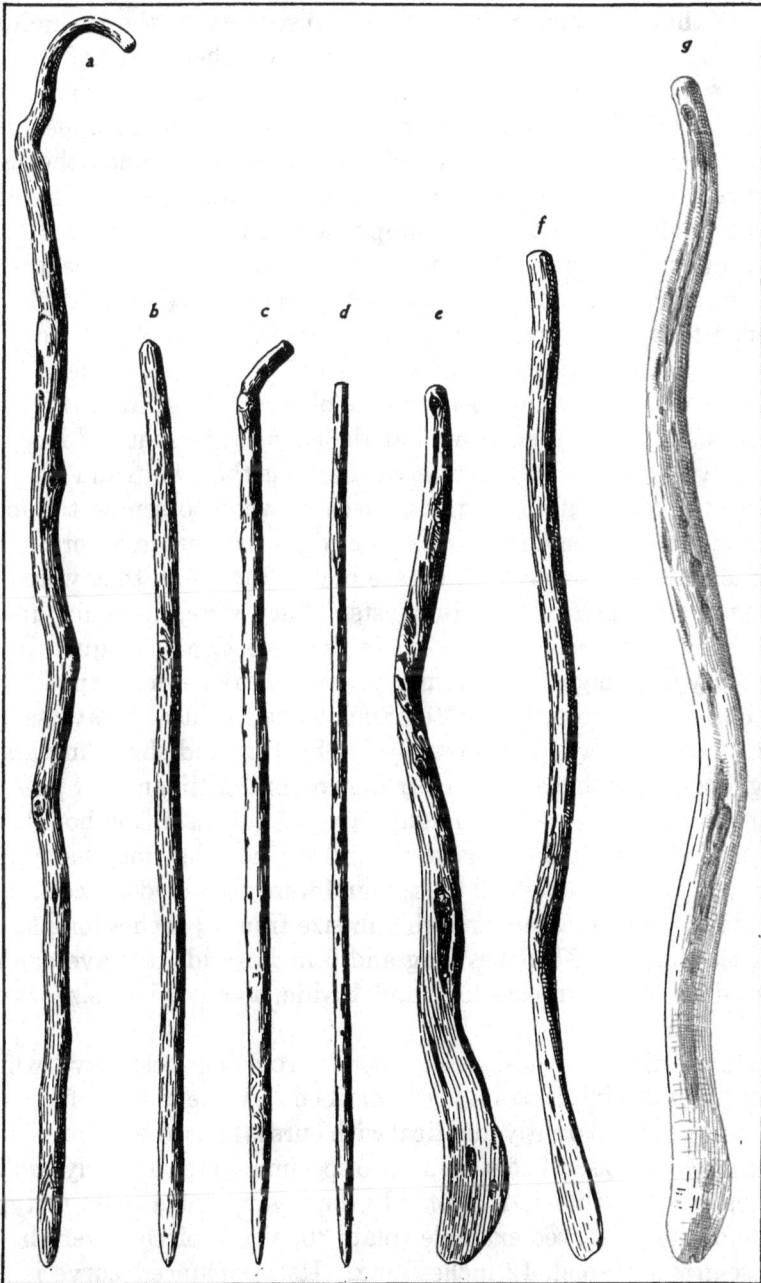

Planting sticks. All from White Dog Cave with the exception of e and f, which are from Cave 7.   (About 1/7.)

caves that we came to regard their discovery in the preliminary examination of a site as an indication that other traces of Basket-maker occupancy would be found. For this reason they are given a more detailed description than their commonplace appearance might seem to warrant. All of them have very much the same general form as those illustrated; this seems due to selection rather than to shaping as they are simply wooden slabs from small logs, the outer or convex surface natural, the inner side and ends usually charred by fire. From this and their appearance as a whole, we judge that they were merely unconsumed pieces of firewood, se-lected, as before stated, on account of their shape. A few, how-ever, show no burning, being shells of wood rifted from the outer part of a timber, then ground at the ends to the required length.

One unvarying feature of these objects is their worn and rounded edges; we once used a similar piece of wood to scrape the loose sand from a cist and found that the edges soon became worn in the same way; for this reason we are inclined to think they were em-ployed principally for digging cists. They were, no doubt, found useful for other purposes, as one in the collection has a quantity of caked yellow pigment adhering to its concave side. Apparently it had been used as a palette. Such slabs might also have served as rude food trays, and possibly for beating and shredding grass, a guess that we hazarded in our first report. Still another possible function for these objects might have been transferring hot stones from the fire to cooking baskets, in which case they may have been used in pairs. Though all those found were not saved the collection contains nineteen pieces ranging in size from 5½ inches long and 3 inches wide to 18½ inches long and 6 inches wide, the average di-mensions being 7 inches long and 4 wide, a convenient size to use in the hand.

Hough figures " a shell of wood " from Tularosa cave which resembles the implements just described;[1] while another from the Mesa Verde apparently identical with ours is figured by Morris.[2]

Curved Wooden Tools. Our two specimens are so closely similar to each other that it is probable they represent a definite type. The better preserved example (plate 36, a) is a piece of very hard, close-grained wood, 12 inches long. Its pronounced curve is ap-parently natural, but all its surfaces have been worked down by

[1] Hough, 1914, plate 14, figure 2.　　　[2] Morris, 1919, a; plate 44, e.

whittling or scraping. One end is almost round, the other much thinner. The middle part of the concave side is worn to a slim rounded edge and is highly polished by long use. The two ends are stained dark by much handling. The object was obviously held by the ends and worked toward the body like a modern drawknife. The unscratched condition and high polish of the concave edge shows that it must have been used on some non-abrasive substance. Its curve fits the thigh so well that we have thought the implement might have been employed in some way for dressing or suppling hides held over the knee.

The second specimen, though a trifle longer, is of the same shape and bears the same polish on the inner edge.

Other Objects of Wood. On plate 41, a, is illustrated a pair of slim worked twigs, $7\frac{1}{2}$ inches long and $\frac{3}{16}$ of an inch in diameter. The two are held together by a string tied in little grooves that encircle their lower ends; this is evidently a permanent attachment but it is loose enough to allow the two sticks to be spread apart. An adjustable tie was evidently used at the upper end, for there only one twig is grooved and the other has a small hole drilled through it. A string is made fast to the grooved stick; its loose end was undoubtedly passed through the hole, pulled tight and made fast when it was desired to close the pair together and hold them in place. A number of similar objects are in the Grand Gulch collection in the American Museum, New York (H–13180 and H–13267); these sticks are also tied permanently together at their lower ends, and have a loose-ended string set in a groove at the upper end of one of them. The other stick, in each of the New York pairs, has a little string loop instead of the drilled eye of the example here illustrated. All these specimens were evidently designed to be clamped over and made fast about objects 6 or 7 inches wide and not over $\frac{1}{4}$ of an inch thick. As to what such objects might have been we are entirely ignorant. A wooden awl about 6 inches long, made from a peeled greasewood stick, was found; the butt is cut off square and the other end is whittled to a sharp point. For a variety of other specimens made wholly or in part of wood, see under "Ceremonial Objects."

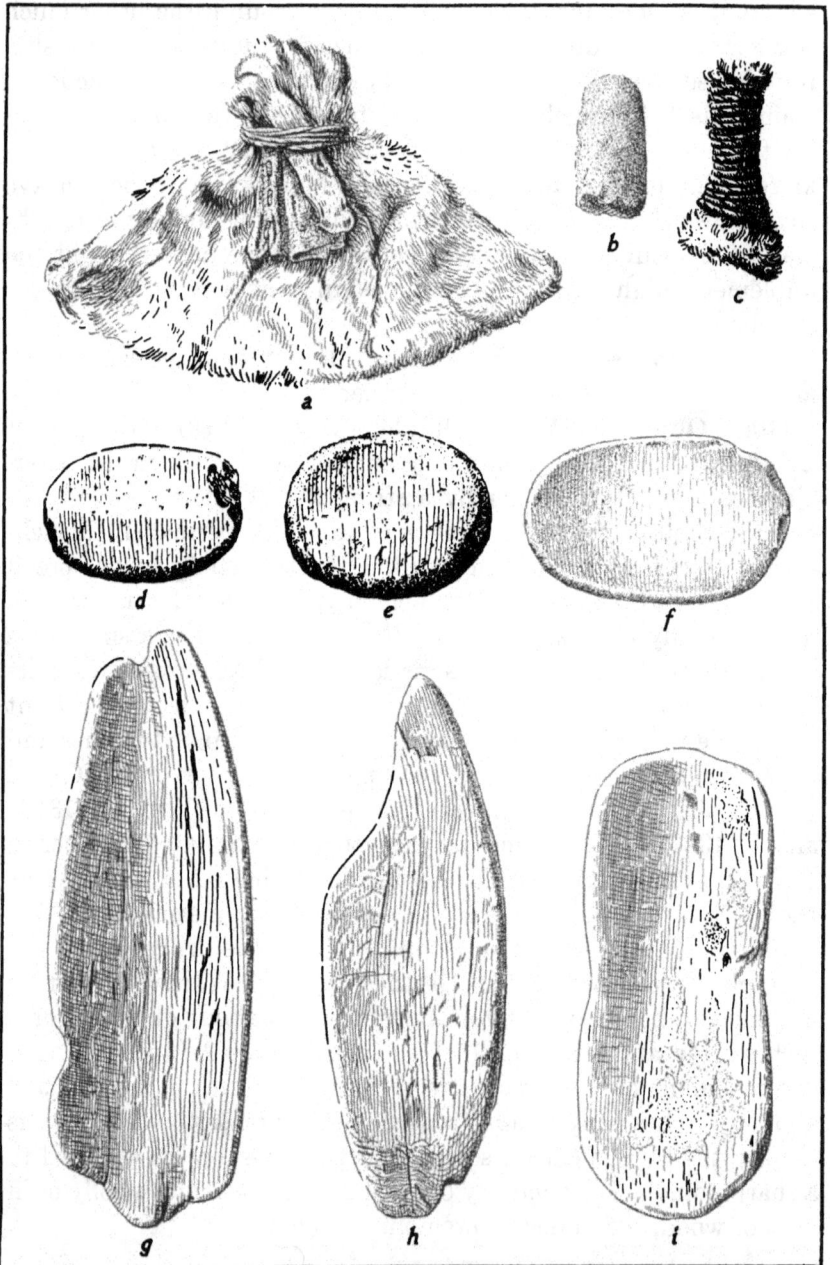

a, b, c, Skin bag and contents; d, e, f, Manos or grinding stones; g, h, i, Wooden scoops.
a, b, c, Cave 14; d–i, White Dog Cave. (About ½.)

OBJECTS OF STONE

Manos. These are intimately related to the domestic life of corn-growing Indians, and in a measure furnish an index to their progress as agriculturists. The manos of the more highly developed tribes, such as the Pueblos, show a tendency towards specialized forms; while those used by people of less firmly established corn-eating habits are as a rule stones of convenient shape with little or no alteration of the original form other than that due to wear. Basket-maker manos belong to the latter class. Three typical examples from White Dog Cave are reproduced in plate 38, d, e, f.

The latter is 5¾ inches long, 3½ inches wide, and 1¼ inches thick. It is made from a thin slab of indurated sandstone the edges roughly worked down to give the implement an oval shape. Only one surface shows use, this is ground nearly flat. The one figured in d, is 3¾ inches long, 2¾ inches wide and 1¾ inches thick; it is a hard lava-like stone of natural shape. One side is much worn and has a convex surface; a small area of the top also shows signs of use. That shown in e, is slightly larger than the last and of the same material. The form shows slight modification and both sides are about equally worn.

In addition to the above specimens, there is in the collection half a mano of soft sandstone with edges pecked and ground to give it an oval shape. Both sides are much worn; one shows traces of a dark red, the other of a yellow color, presumably evidences of secondary use as a paint grinder. Another stone of about the same size but which is probably not a mano, is a rounded river boulder 4½ inches long and 2½ inches thick. A portion of either side bears a high polish quite different from the rough surface produced by grinding on a metate. This polish is obviously the result of long rubbing on a non-abrasive surface; work on hides or use in hulling seeds in a basket may be suggested.

Metate. A single broken specimen was found. Like the manos it is of a crude and unspecialized type, being merely a flat slab unmodified except for a hollow on one side, the width of which is the same as the length of the manos.

Chipped Knife Blades. One of these specimens (plate 35, j) was found at the right hand of mummy 2, Cist 27, White Dog Cave.

Its length is $6\frac{7}{8}$ inches, its greatest width is $2\frac{7}{8}$ inches, the average thickness is $\frac{1}{4}$ of an inch. The material is a mottled yellow flint. The point for $1\frac{1}{2}$ inches is a dark red which seems due to staining rather than being the natural color of the stone. It was reduced to an even thinness by the chipping off at regular intervals of long broad flakes, at so obtuse an angle that no central ridge is left, the face of the blade being slightly convex instead of angular. The cutting edge is keen, the result of fine secondary chipping. The stem is tapered to a wedge-shaped base.

The blade shown in k was found with mummy 3, Cist 22. It had been broken in two pieces before burial; the halves lay at a little distance from each other and one of them was discolored by some agency to which the other was not exposed. This blade measures $6\frac{1}{2}$ inches in length, $2\frac{1}{2}$ inches in width, and averages slightly under $\frac{1}{4}$ of an inch in thickness. The material is chalcedony. It differs but little from the first specimen, except that the end is rounded and shows signs of an attempt to grind away a slight protuberance that had resisted the original chipping. On the base of the blade are traces of the gum that once served to cement it to its haft. The latter was also found in the cist; and although it is badly rotted and shrunken, its notch still fits the blade. In shape it is a duplicate of the haft next to be described.

The workmanship of these two knives compares very favorably with that of similar implements from other parts of North America. In shape and general appearance they most closely resemble the large chipped knives of Mexico and Central America.

Hafted Knife. The specimen shown in plate 35, l, is from Cist 6, White Dog Cave. The blade, part of which is unfortunately missing, was probably once $4\frac{1}{2}$ to 5 inches long; it is 2 inches wide at the base and has a thickness of $\frac{1}{4}$ inch. The material is a close-grained white stone. The chipping of the portion that remains is rather coarse, though the notches and barbs show skillful flaking.

The wooden handle measures $3\frac{1}{4}$ inches in length, a fraction over 1 inch in width, and has an average thickness of $\frac{3}{8}$ of an inch. The lower end thickens considerably to allow for a notch $\frac{3}{4}$ of an inch deep into which the blade is set and there held in place with cement-like gum reinforced by a small wooden wedge and wrappings of pitch-smeared string. The handle is well-preserved and shows careful finish; it appears to have been made from a section of a small

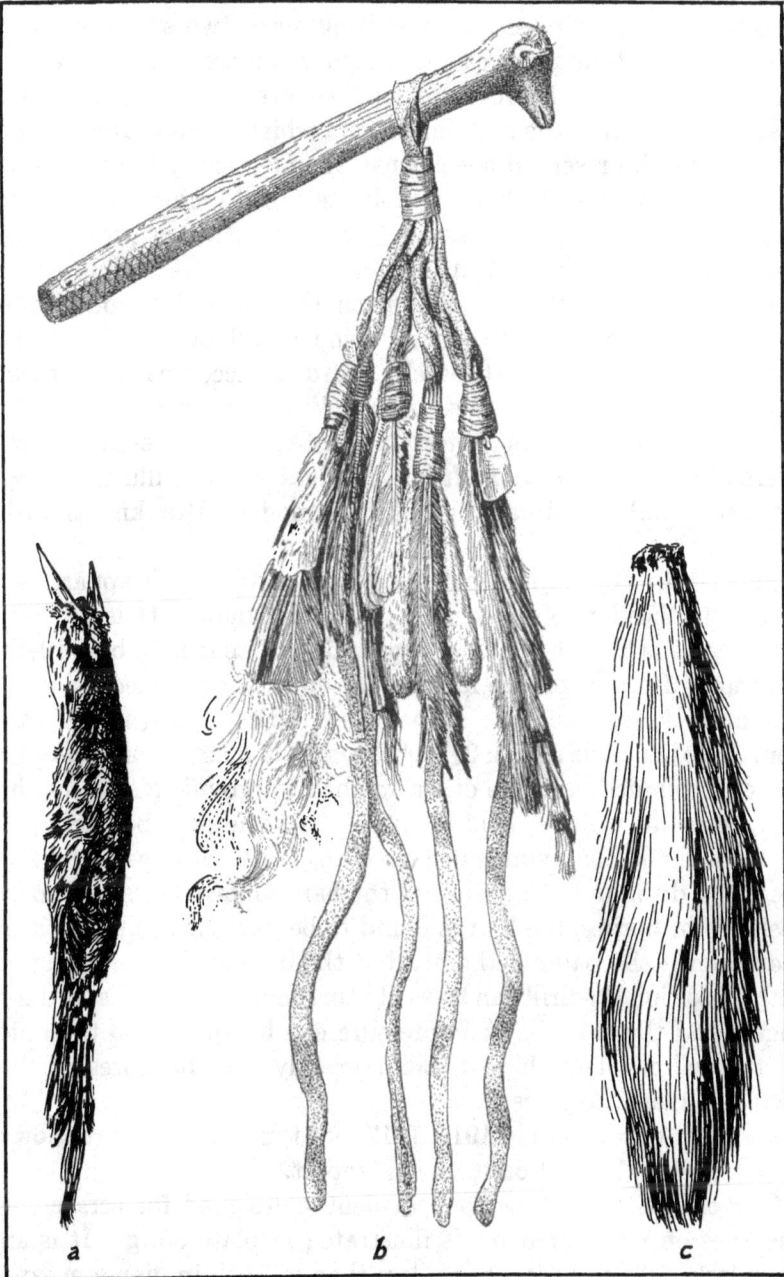

WHITE DOG CAVE
Ceremonial objects: a, Stuffed bird skin; b, Wand; c, Deer tail.   (About 3/5.)

limb worked down to shape by cutting away two surfaces; both the wide sides thus produced are slightly convex, while the edges are nearly flat. At the butt the handle curves and terminates in a neatly finished end, the peculiar form of which is duplicated in two other less well-preserved specimens; one of them is the handle of the large chipped blade, k, previously described. This type of butt may represent an individual whim, or it may perhaps prove to be a characteristic of Basket-maker hafts. There are a number of stone knives with plain handles from this general region in the collections of various museums; some or all of these may be Basket-maker, but unfortunately the data accompanying them leave doubt as to their exact origin. What are, however, surely Cliff-dweller hafts from Aztec, New Mexico, are described and figured by Morris,[1] and one from the Mesa Verde is illustrated by Nordenskiold.[2] Hoffman figures two modern Ute knives with plain handles.[3]

Pipe Drill. The chipped point shown in plate 35, e, is apparently an old darthead remounted in its present handle. It is of very hard, lustrous flint, $1\frac{5}{16}$ inches long, and $\frac{3}{16}$ of an inch in breadth at the base. Both edges are much worn down and beveled by long-continued boring, the plane of the bevels indicating clockwise rotation. The handle is a stick $2\frac{3}{4}$ inches long, $\frac{3}{8}$ of an inch thick, having one end rounded, and the other notched to provide a seat for the chipped point, which is held in place by a seizing of fiber string.

The wear on the point indicates clearly that this specimen was used as a drill, and the nature of the haft confirms this. Held in position for boring, the haft is found to be just the right length to bear against the palm of the hand at the base of the index finger; in this position the drill can be easily turned by the index and third fingers and the thumb, while pressure can be applied to the butt by the palm. The chipped point exactly fits the bores of the Basket-maker stub pipes.

No pipes were found in 1916–1917, but type examples are shown in figure 94, a, b, c, of our previous report.

Graver. A tiny stone tool, evidently designed for scratching fine lines on wood or bone, is illustrated in plate 35, g. It is an irregularly shaped jasper flake, less than an inch in diameter, and $\frac{3}{16}$ of an inch thick; the top is convex; the lower side is flat at one

---

[1] 1919, p. 33 and figures 17, 18.   [2] 1893, p. 97, figure 59.   [3] 1896, figures 52, 53.

place where a small and very sharp point has been carefully chipped out. Such an implement as this must have been used to incise the clean-cut parallel lines seen on the curved wooden clubs figured on plate 36, f, g.

Flaking Tool. This implement (figure 15) from plundered Cist 6, White Dog Cave, is included here because of its intimate connection with stone chipping. So far as we know it is the only complete example of a prehistoric flaker of its type that has yet been found. It consists of an antler or very hard bone point mounted on a wooden shaft in the manner indicated in the drawing, which also shows more clearly than a description the shape of the point itself. The length of the latter is $3\frac{3}{4}$ inches, of which $\frac{5}{16}$ of an inch projects beyond the end of the shaft; the width appears to be uniformly $\frac{1}{4}$ of an inch. The projecting portion tapers to $\frac{1}{8}$ of an inch at the extreme end. The shaft is a piece of an old atlatl spear shaft 35 inches long. The bone point is bound to the smaller end of this by seizings of skin overwrapped with sinew. The larger end is worked to a rounded point, for the purpose, perhaps, of allowing it to be easily thrust into the sand to hold it upright while the workman was using other tools. In the middle are a number of turns of a wide thong of skin wound spirally about the shaft and running towards the working end. These are applied in two layers, one above the other; at the distal end they are held in place by a binding of sinew and there are signs that they once extended farther down the shaft than they do at present. These wrappings were probably cut from hide with the hair on it, although the fur has now almost entirely disappeared; their purpose will be discussed later.

There is no doubt that this implement was used as a stone-flaker. Pope figures a Yurok bone pointed arrow-flaker with a shaft $17\frac{3}{4}$ inches long, which is very similar to this specimen.[1] Rau illustrates another from Nevada which he describes as a slender blunt point of horn bound with cotton cord to a wooden handle about the thickness of an arrow shaft. According to the drawing the length of the latter is $29\frac{1}{2}$ inches.[2] Cushing gives a sketch of an arrowmaker using a long-hafted flaker, but provides no information as to the data on which the drawing is based, though he briefly describes the way the implement is used.[3] The following

---

[1] 1918, plate 27.   [2] 1876, p. 96, and figure 340.   [3] 1895, figure 6.

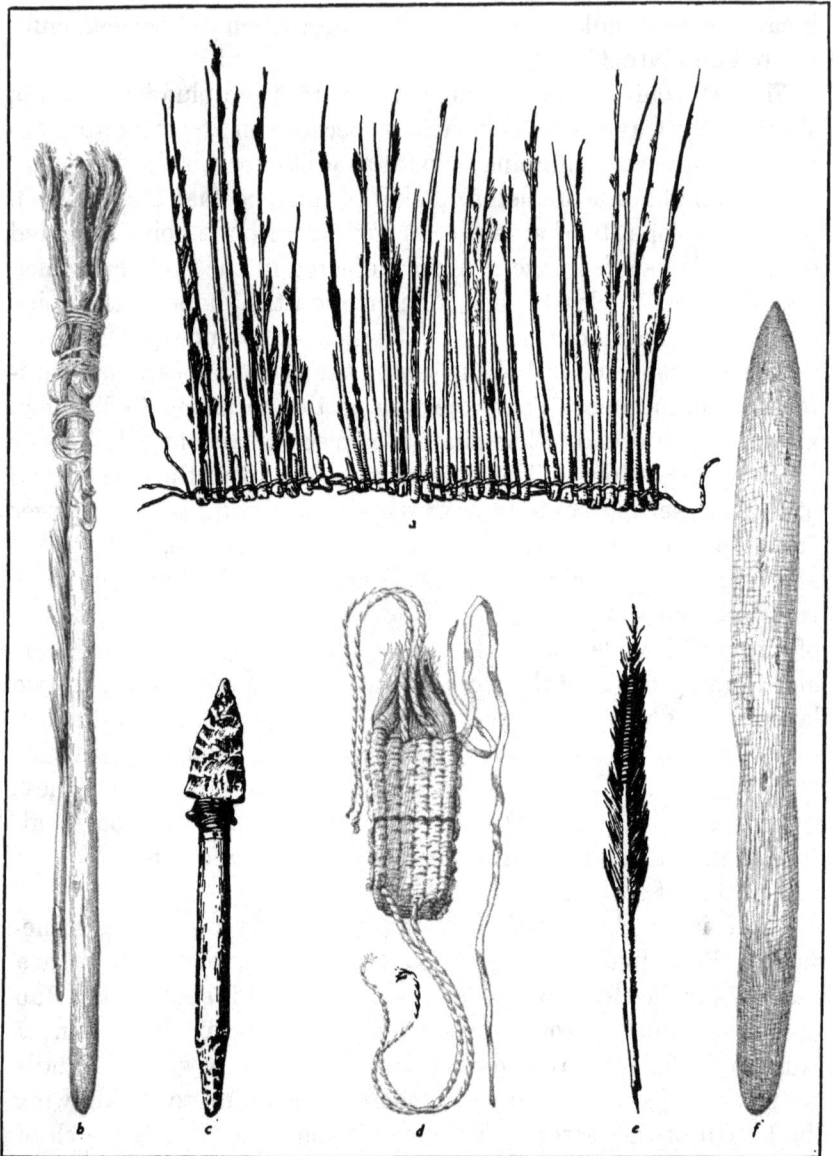

WHITE DOG CAVE
Objects forming bundle from lap of mummy (plate 7, b), Cist 31.　(About ⅓.)

is Schumacher's description of the Klamath method of flaking: "The tool is worked with the right hand, while the lower part of the handle, usually ornamented, is held between the arm and the body so as to guide the instrument with a steady hand."[1] The foregoing makes clear the advantage of the long shaft, but does not point out the fact that the weight of the body can, by means of it, be brought to assist the pressure of the hand.

We can find no reference to padding of that part of the shaft that is held between the arm and body; such was undoubtedly

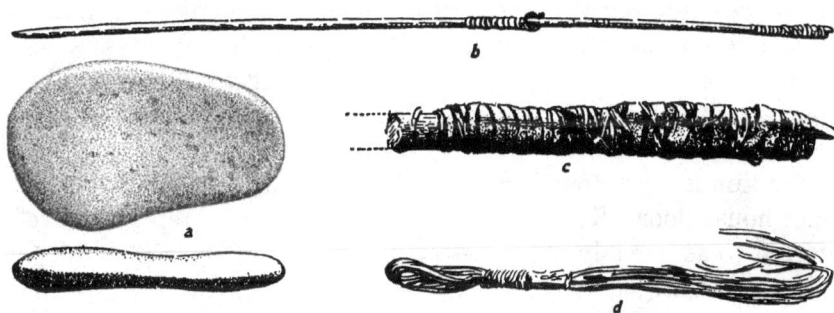

FIGURE 15

a, Flaking stone; b, Arrow-flaker of antler in wooden haft, much reduced in size; c, End of arrow-flaker; d, Package of sinew cord. All from White Dog Cave. (About ⅓, with the exception of b.)

the purpose of the central hide wrappings on our specimen. A soft furry padding of this sort must have contributed greatly to the comfort of the user, particularly if his arm and body were not protected by clothing; and it probably helped also to secure a firmer grip than would be offered by the bare shaft.

Flaking Stone. The specimen shown in a, figure 15, is a small flat unworked stone, oval in outline, 3¾ inches long, 2½ inches wide and ½ inch thick. It is much like certain stones obtained in the Museum's explorations of ancient burial places in Erie County, New York, which were invariably accompanied by bone flaking implements as well as finished and unfinished chipped points and knives. The Museum collection also contains similar stones from Madisonville, Ohio,[2] and eastern Massachusetts. Mr. Willoughby has identified these stones as forming part of the flint worker's equipment. The stones from New York, Ohio, and Massachusetts are marked with scorings which are not present on this specimen;

[1] Quoted in Holmes, 1919, p. 312.   [2] See Hooton and Willoughby, 1920, plate 6, l, m.

our tentative identification of this as a flaking stone is strengthened
by the fact that it was found among the partly rifled contents of
Cist 6 which also held the hafted flaking tool described above, as
well as a small skin bag containing two nearly finished points, a
number of flakes of flint and various colored jasper, a combination
of objects exactly duplicating those found in the New York graves.

OBJECTS OF CLAY, BONE, ETC.

Pottery. No specimens of true pottery, either vessel or sherd,
have yet been found by us under circumstances indicating that it
was a Basket-maker product. All but one of the several jars discovered came from the surface sand overlying the Basket-maker
deposits; they are of common cliff-house ware, and were undoubtedly cached in the caves at a comparatively late date. The
exception is a pot found in Sunflower Cave in 1915, lying below a
cliff-house floor. This was figured in our previous report and referred to as possibly of Basket-maker origin.[1] It is of plain black
ware, uncorrugated; in shape it is almost spherical. No further
evidence that the Basket-makers produced vessels of this type
has since come to light, and we are inclined to consider it early
Puebloan.

The only specimen that even remotely resembles pottery was
found in Cave 6. It is a fragment from the rim of a shallow dish-
like receptacle nearly ½ inch thick, made of unburned clay heavily
tempered with shreds of cedar bark. It was molded in a shallow
basket, the print of which is plainly visible in the outer surface of
the sherd (plate 25, a). The inner side is smoothed off, but has an
irregular, wavy surface as if it had been done by the fingers. We
do not know whether this specimen is merely a fragment of a clay
lining put in a basket to render it watertight or fireproof,[2] or
whether it really represents an early attempt at pottery making.

Bone Objects. Objects of this material described under other
heads are: beads, flaker, decorated tubes, rattle handles, plain
tubes, and whistles. This practically completes the list of specimens made of bone, the only others being a few awls (plate 42,
e–h), and a pair of unworked cannon bones of the deer, found

---

[1] Kidder-Guernsey, 1919, plate 59, a, and p. 144.

[2] Cushing (1886, p. 484) describes a Havasupai roasting basket lined with clay. The present
object may have been made for a like purpose, but it was certainly never so used, as bits of the
cedar-bark tempering which protrude from the inner surface are not even scorched.

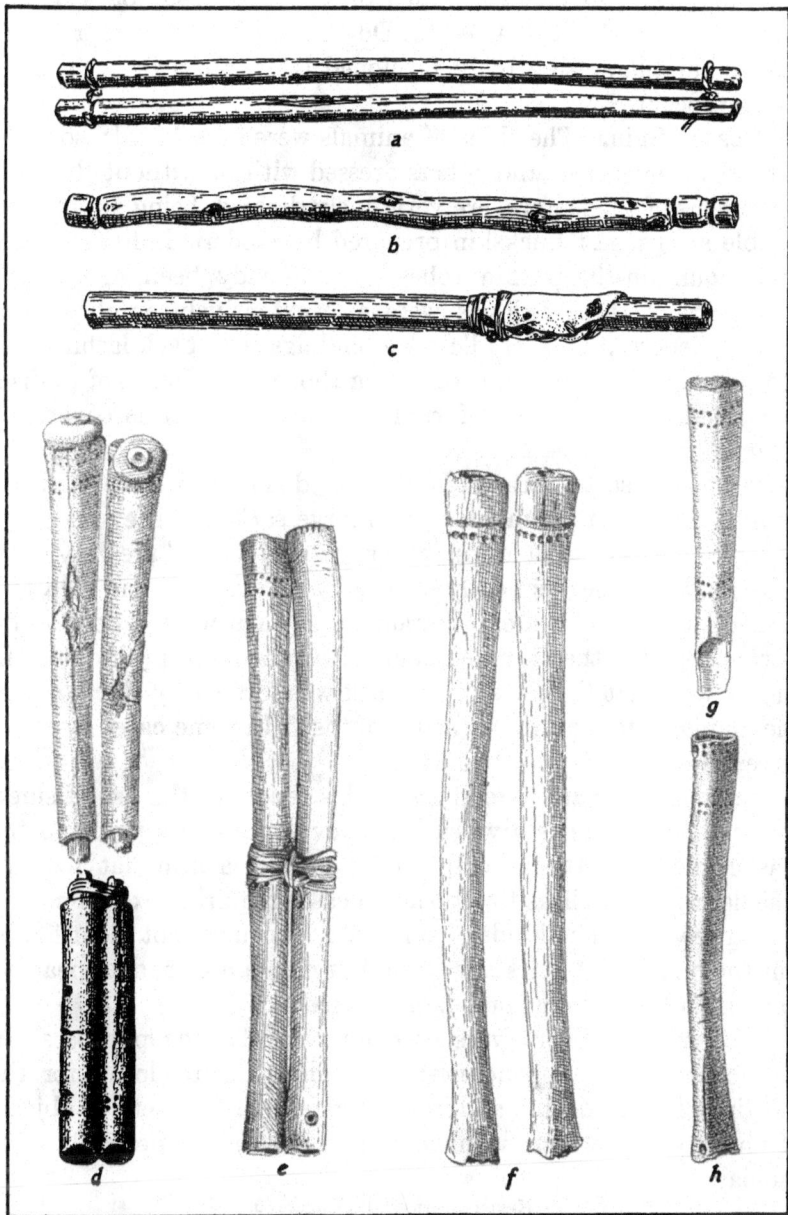

a, b, c, Objects made from short sections of sticks; d, e, f, Paired bone tubes; g, h, Bone tubes. All from White Dog Cave except f, which is from Sunflower Cave. (About ½.)

carefully wrapped up in a bunch of shredded cedar bark at the feet of mummy 1, Cist 24, White Dog Cave. These were probably selected and laid aside to be fashioned later into awls. No bone scrapers occur.

Dressed Skin. The skins of animals were much used: some as rawhide, some dried, and others dressed with or without the hair. Specimens of the latter were very finely dressed, being as soft and pliable as the best buckskin prepared by modern Indians. Deer and mountain-sheep skin robes have already been mentioned. The pelts of these animals were also extensively employed for minor purposes, as in cradle edge-bindings and back-lashings, in fur-string, and for all kinds of strong thongs. The skins of prairie-dogs, being light and soft-furred were always used as covers for infants' umbilical pads.

Bags of all sorts were made of dressed skin, from tiny pouches to hold a few little trinkets, up to large sacks for the storage of corn. Some have the hair on, others do not; but all are very carefully made, the seams neatly stitched with sinew or fine cord and turned inside. The most characteristic bags were produced by sewing together the trimmed skins of two or more prairie-dogs in such a way that the neck of the sack was formed by the heads of the animals, its mouth by their mouths.[1] In some cases as many as seven or eight hides were used.

Sinew. The many references in this report to the use of sinew bindings and seizings give sufficient evidence of its value to the Basket-makers. It was employed whenever a firm flat ligature was desired, as well as for thread in cases requiring extra fine and strong sewing. The kinds of sinew are, of course, not identifiable, but the bunch of it in its raw state shown in figure 15, d, appears to have been taken from some large animal.

Feathers. Feathers were used for the following purposes: in hair ornaments; in pendants; as edgings in fur cloth; for the winging of atlatl darts; and in the make-up of a variety of objects of unknown use which we have classed together as probably ceremonial.

[1] Kidder-Guernsey, 1919, figure 86.

CEREMONIAL OBJECTS

In this section we have grouped all specimens to which we cannot assign a definite utilitarian purpose. The nature of many of them leaves little doubt as to their ceremonial or fetishistic use; as to others the case is less clear.

Ceremonial Whip. To one end of a thin, peeled greasewood stick about 20 inches in length there is bound a flat, three-strand braid of shredded yucca leaves, 8 inches long; to the end of this is tied a small bunch of the twigs of the plant called " Brigham tea" ; the twigs are 10 inches long, so that the total length of the specimen is a little over a yard. It has the look of a scourge or whip, but its real use is, of course, unknown.

Problematical Objects. In Cist 27, White Dog Cave, were found a number of broken sticks tied together with string. On undoing the bundle it was found that the sticks were fragments of two singular contrivances, the use of which we cannot .even guess (plate 36, d, e). One is complete, the upper part of the second is missing. They are slim cottonwood sticks about 7 feet long, their lower ends pointed, and the first foot or so of their shafts soiled and scarred as if they had been repeatedly thrust into gravelly earth. The arrangement of strings at the upper end of the complete specimen is better explained by the drawing than by description. It will be seen that there are two cords running downward from the tip. These are so arranged as to form two adjustable loops along the shaft, the knotted ends of the strings serving to keep these loops from being pulled out by whatever object they were designed to hold.

The object shown in c, is a hardwood branch 27¼ inches long. The bark has been carefully peeled and the butt end smoothed by rubbing. For a distance of about 4 inches from the butt the twigs have been cut off close to the main stem; thence to the tip they are also cut off, but their bases have been left long enough to give the object a knobby appearance. The ends of a majority of these protruding twig-stubs are merely ground down to a flat surface; but three, two of which show in the drawing, have neat, shallow, cup-shaped depressions worked in them. The lower four inches of the stick, from which, it will be remembered, the projecting twig-stubs were removed, is discolored and stained as if by having been

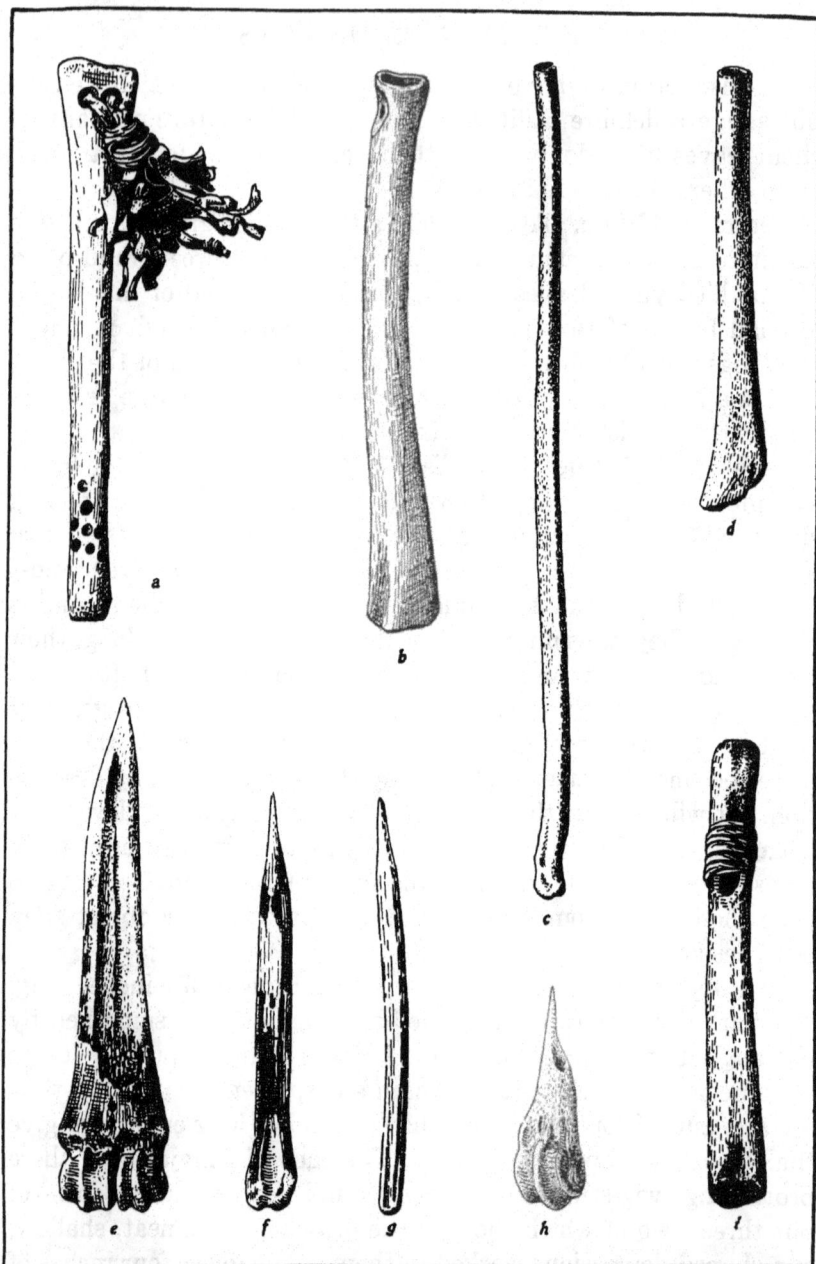

WHITE DOG CAVE

a, Handle for deer-hoof rattle; b, c, d, Bone tubes; e–h, Bone awls; i, Bone whistle.   (½.)

thrust into damp earth or clay. A little above the middle are two sets of sinew bindings; under the upper one of these are remains of the quills of many small feathers arranged in two groups, one on either side of the shaft. We can offer no suggestion as to the use of this specimen.

Ceremonial Wand. The unique ceremonial object shown in plate 39, b, was found with mummy 2, Cist 24, White Dog Cave; it was wrapped in a bag made of prairie-dog skins, and lay between the right arm and side of the mummy under the fur-string robe which enveloped the body. Details that are not obvious in the drawing are as follows: the handle of wood has a length of 5⅛ inches; the upper end is carved to represent the head of a bird; the eyes are formed by two small disk beads of shell stuck on with pitch. Adhering to the head about the eyes are tufts of the fine reddish hair of some animal. At the crown of the head there is a slight depression filled with hard gum or pitch in which are a few hairs like those at the side of the head. These may be the remains of a crest, or the result of accident. The appearance of the spot gives the impression that some object about the size of the disk beads which form the eyes, had at one time been fastened here. At the lower end of the handle its under side is embellished for a space of slightly over 1½ inches with cross hatching of fine incised lines. All parts of the handle are nicely finished, and show, particularly at the lower end, a polish due to use. Attached to it by a thong loop are five pendent strings or streamers of thick soft-dressed skin; part of one of these is broken off, the remaining four are each 10 inches in length. These streamers are gathered together at the upper end and secured to the loop by wrappings of sinew. Bound to the upper end of each streamer by sinew seizings are tails of small birds and animals, and feathers. One streamer has five blue feathers, five small brown feathers, and one white and brown feather; the next, one long downy feather, one large dark-colored feather trimmed off at the end and several small brown feathers. The third has the quill ends of two large dark-colored feathers; these are cut down to a length of 3 inches, and placed parallel to each other with the lower ends fastened together by several tight turns of fine sinew; over these are laid a number of small bright yellow feathers; a strand of human hair 3 inches long completes the group. The fourth streamer has fastened to it six feathers from the tail of some small woodpecker, and two prairie-dog tails. The fifth bears several blue feathers, one trimmed black-and-white feather, the tail of a small animal, the fur of which is about the color of mink, and a very pretty little abalone shell pendant.

The specimen just described, like a number of objects recovered from Cist 24, is in a nearly perfect state of preservation. Wrapped up with it was the small deer tail shown in c, the head of a sap-sucker (*Splegrapicus varius muchalis*)[1] a, and what appears to be the end of a bag made of badger skin dressed with the hair on. The bird head is stuffed with fiber or grass, and the tail feathers of the bird, tied together in a bundle, are thrust into the skin of the neck. A Pomo doctor's outfit in the Museum collection contains a number of bird heads stuffed with grass which remind one at once of this specimen.

Ceremonial Bundle. In plate 7, b, can be seen what is doubtless a ceremonial bundle, one end resting in the lap of the mummy, the other projecting above the left knee, this being the position in which it was found.

In the center of the bundle lay a wand-like stick, $14\frac{1}{2}$ inches long, which is shown in b, plate 40. One end has a blunt point, is slightly polished for an inch or more, and is stained a dark red color; the opposite end is rounded and shows traces of fire. To one side of the blunt end and projecting beyond is tied a brush-like arrangement of coarse fiber also stained dark red. The same string which binds the fiber to the stick secures to it a long feather of which there remains very little but the shaft. Other articles tied about the stick and figured in the plate, are as follows:

The curious object, shown in d, more nearly resembles a minia-ture sandal than anything else, being of the same weave as a cer-tain type of Basket-maker sandal. The strings attached to it are not, however, arranged like sandal tie-strings. There is a dressed skin thong, colored red, woven into one end; this may be an un-finished toe-fringe. The specimen is 4 inches long, and $1\frac{1}{2}$ inches wide. The material is fiber string, except the dark line through the center which is of human hair string.

The blade-like object of tough, close-grained wood shown in f, is $12\frac{1}{4}$ inches long, $1\frac{1}{8}$ inches wide, and $\frac{3}{8}$ to $\frac{5}{8}$ of an inch thick.

[1] Identified by Mr. O. Bangs of the Museum of Comparative Zoölogy, Harvard University.

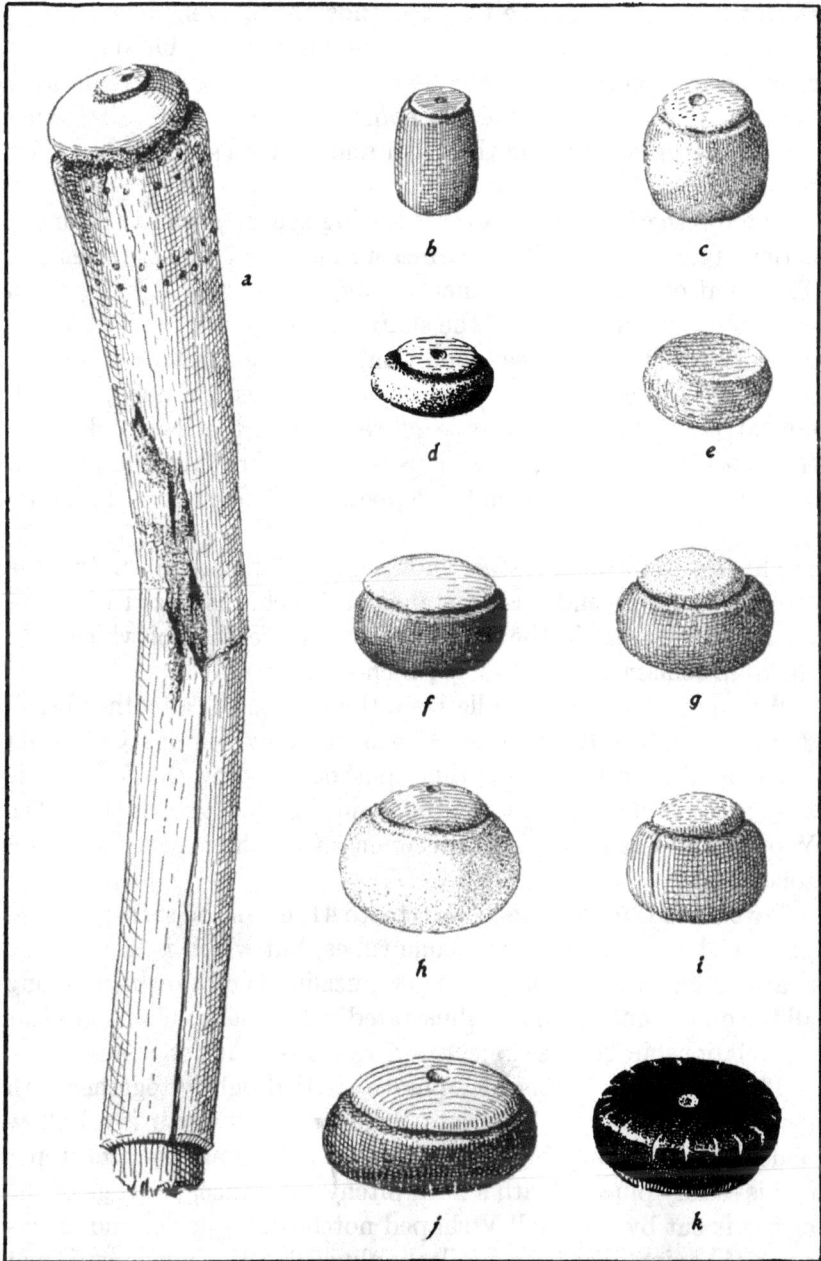

WHITE DOG CAVE

a, One of a pair of bone tubes showing compound die cemented to upper end;
b–k, Compound dice.   (Enlarged 1/5.)

Both the pointed and the rounded ends are blackened as a result of shaping or hardening by fire. The edges of the blunt end are rounded for something over a hand's breadth; for the remaining distance to the beginning of the point both edges are sharp. One edge is rather keener than the other and shows a surface smoothed by wear.

The foreshaft and point of a throwing spear c, from the bundle is the largest in our collection, measuring over 7 inches in length. The point of red jasper, $2\frac{1}{4}$ inches long, 1 inch wide at base, is set in a notch cut in the end of the shaft and secured by a sinew binding which is still in perfect condition, as is the shaft itself except for traces of decay at the tapering end. This specimen, though our largest, is not as long as the foreshafts in the Lang collection from San Juan County, Utah, now in the Deseret Museum, which, according to the table given by Pepper,[1] are $7\frac{1}{4}$ inches to $11\frac{1}{4}$ inches in length.

The tips of the long feather shown in e, is 7 inches in length; the quill at its upper end for a distance of 2 inches is seized with fine flat sinew as shown in the drawing. Another feather, of which only the quill remains, measured $15\frac{3}{4}$ inches in length.

Wrapped about the bundle were the remains of a feather headdress not unlike the feather crowns used by various California tribes in their ceremonies. The method of tying the feathers is shown in the illustration, a; the same knot is also used by the Wailaki and Shasta Indians, specimens of which are in the Museum collection.

Ceremonial Bone Objects. In plate 41, e, will be seen what appears to be merely a pair of bone tubes, but which is in reality a nearly complete example of a very puzzling type to which belong all the other bone specimens illustrated in the plate. To make clear the relationship of these objects a detailed description is necessary.

The two halves of this contrivance are tied tightly together with a strip of yucca leaf. The right-hand unit of the pair is a hollow bone, $6\frac{5}{8}$ inches long, highly polished as if by long use; its upper end is solidly plugged with a dark pitchy substance, the edge of the orifice is cut by six small V-shaped notches; the lower end shows signs of having once been similarly plugged, but is now open; just above the orifice there are two small round holes, drilled directly

[1] Pepper, 1905, p. 129.

146

opposite each other (only one shows in the drawing). The left-hand unit is made up of two bones of equal length fastened to each other by being pushed together over a round stick which fits very tightly in their hollow interiors; the joint is further secured by a sinew cord laced back and forth through series of little holes drilled close to the edge of each bone (three of these holes may be made out in the drawing, the rest are hidden by the main yucca leaf binding). Just below the upper end of this compound bone are two horizontal lines of small round pits, or incised dots; these only run half way around and do not appear on the back. The end of the lower piece is pierced on one side by a small hole, and just above the orifice there is scratched a single encircling line. Neither end of the left-hand unit gives any indication of having been plugged as were both orifices of the right-hand bone.

The fragments of the specimen shown in d, are assembled in what were doubtless their original positions. They form a pair very similar to the one just described, but both halves are compound, each being made up of two pieces once held together by an interior stick or dowel. Parts of a main binding that once fastened the two halves to each other are still preserved. The lower part of the left-hand unit has on one side three deep horizontal notches and a single small round hole; the upper piece has three double lines of incised dots which, as in the preceding specimen, only run half way around. The right-hand unit has two similar double lines of dots, one near the bottom, one just below the top. The upper end of each unit is plugged with pitch, in which are set the curious compound objects shown in the drawing. They are flattened spheres of red stone with small, white, perforated discs glued to their tops. The right-hand sphere has been somewhat warped from its original flat position across the end of the bone.

The pair of tubes shown in f, were found together in Sunflower Cave and illustrated in our first report (plate 86, f); they are reproduced here because they are surely of the same nature as the White Dog Cave specimens. They fit snugly when laid side by side and show, indeed, signs of rubbing along the points of contact; hence they once were undoubtedly bound together. Near the upper end of each one, and running only half way around,[1] is an

[1] In our first description we mistakenly stated that the dots encircled the bones (Kidder-Guernsey, 1919, p. 189).

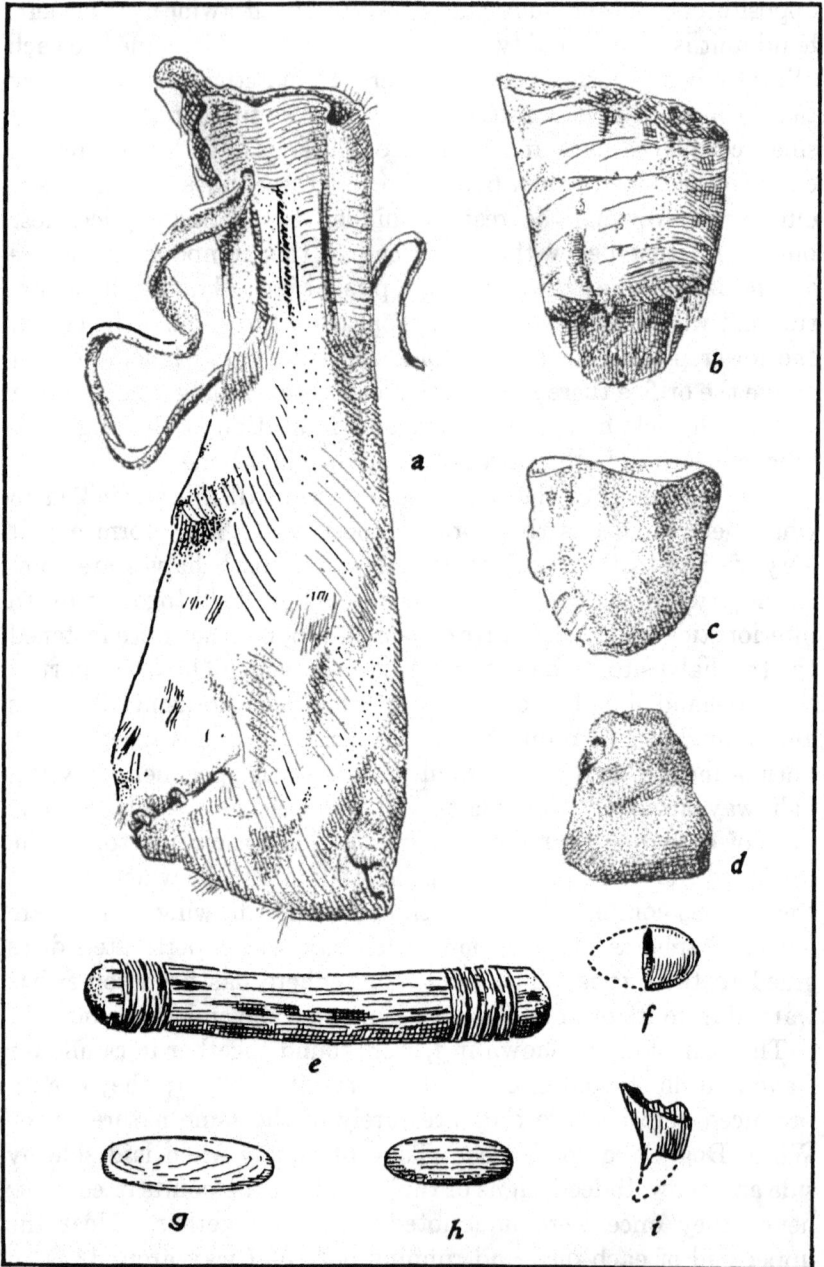

CAVE 6

a–d, Skin pouch and objects found with it in woven bag; e–i, Articles from within pouch. (About 4/5.)

incised line and a row of dots. If pitch was ever used to plug up these bones, it has entirely disappeared.

Two other bone objects (g and h) are fragments which obviously formed parts of pairs identical with the above. They are of the same general shape and size, and have similar rows of small dots only partially encircling them. The upper one, g, is the best preserved of several fragments of a broken specimen; found loose in the same cist with it were four compound " buttons " very like the ones glued to the ends of the pair shown in d.

To sum up: these objects were pairs of bones tied together at the middle; the component parts of each pair might be a single bone, or might be made of two bones fastened end to end. All are decorated with lines of dots, and many, perhaps all, had at one place or another small drilled holes. Some at least were provided with compound " buttons " glued to their ends. The fact that the incised dots never completely encircle the bones, and that the undotted surface of each bone is always the flatter side, seems to indicate that these assemblages were held or worn against something in such a position that one side was not visible. We have only one hint as to a possible use; lying close against the central ligature of the pair figured in d, and apparently engaged by it (the specimen is badly rotted) was a cord hung with nearly a hundred deer-hoofs. The latter may have formed a rattle, and if so, the double bones might perhaps have been some sort of handle for it.

Included here because they were found in the same cists with some of the pairs just described, are two specimens that seem to have served as handles for what we suppose to have been ceremonial wands.[1] The first (plate 42, a) came from the same cist that held the broken paired bones above described. It is a hollow bone, 5¾ inches long, the lower end carefully finished, smoothed, and decorated with eight circular cup-like depressions filled flush with black gum. At the upper end it is perforated by two holes through which runs a narrow thong holding a number of other thongs; the ends of such of the latter as are not broken off are knotted about the remains of the butts of small feathers; the ends of the others are simply knotted. The second specimen, b, from the same cist as e and h, plate 41, is a plain tube with a single hole at one end; its similarity to the above handle is obvious.

---

[1] Compare the bird-headed wooden handle with feathered streamers, plate 39.

Bone Whistle. The specimen illustrated in plate 42, i, was found with the handle last mentioned, one of the complete pairs of bones, and one fragmentary one. Its length is $4\frac{1}{2}$ inches. The lower end is tightly closed with gum, the upper is unsealed. The single rather large opening is partly covered by wrappings of sinew; these seem to have held a bit of reed or other substance, now almost rotted away.

Bone Tubes. The tubes shown in c and d, are both simple lengths of hollow bones with carefully cut ends. They are figured here because we are unable to assign any definite utilitarian function to them.

Compound "Dice." The extremely well-made little objects shown on plate 43, are all from White Dog Cave. Each consists of two parts: a spherical or cylindrical body with rounded bottom and flat top; and a cap, which is a thin disc (often a reused bead with the perforation plugged with pitch) firmly cemented to the flat top of the body. The variety of materials used in their manufacture will be brought out in the descriptions which follow.

The upper and lower sides of the largest example we have is shown in j, k; it measures $\frac{3}{4}$ of an inch in diameter. The body, of highly polished lignite, is perforated vertically, but the hole is carefully plugged; about the lower edge there runs a series of little cuts. The cap is a fine grained red slate disc-bead, the perforation filled with pitch. This specimen, the only one in the lot which was found singly, came from Cist 52.

One of a set of four from Cist 22, is shown in h. It has a translucent quartz body and a cap of red slate. The other three (not figured) are of lignite; one has an unperforated white bone cap, the caps of the remaining two are missing, but dried cement on the flat tops of the bodies proves that they were once present.

A set of seven was found in a small buckskin pouch in Cist 24. One of these, i, has a dark brown wooden base and a white bone cap; a second, f, has a lignite base with an unusually large white limestone cap; the one shown in g, has a lignite base and a light brown stone cap; b, has a long cylindrical base of lignite and a cap of hard light green stone (not turquoise); the fifth (not figured), a lignite base, and light brown stone cap. The sixth, d, and seventh are of a very peculiar construction which was not suspected until one of them accidentally split in halves. It proved to have been made

150

by rolling up a tiny pellet of gray clay mixed with grains of crushed azurite and malachite. Around this pellet was added a thin layer of the same mixture, then another and another like the coats of an onion, until the requisite size and shape of the base were attained. The whole was then daubed with pure gray clay, so that the blue and green particles, so thickly sown through the whole interior, do not show on the surface. The cap of the one figured is a flat green stone, that of the split specimen is of red slate; both are about the same size.

A second set of seven, also contained in a buckskin bag, was taken from Cist 24. These are not figured. Two are of lignite with unperforated brown stone caps; four are of the peculiar azurite-malachite-clay composition, the caps of two are missing. Of the two in place one is a perforated brown stone disc, the other an unperforated disc of green stone. The seventh is beautifully shaped from hematite, it lacks the cap, but, as in all such cases, distinct traces of the cement that once held it in place remain.

Two of another set of seven found loose in Cist 27 are also illustrated in plate 43. The one shown in c, is a hard, light green stone with a cap of white bone; e, is of serpentine and lacks the cap. Of the remaining five, one is sandstone of thin cylindrical form; like e, the cap is missing; the other three have green stone bases with bone, pink stone, and red stone caps respectively.

The purpose of these pretty and beautifully made little things is unknown. Two of them were found glued to the ends of bones (plates 41, d, and 43, a), and the set of four above described came from a disturbed cist (6) which contained fragments of similar paired bones. We at first thought that all such " buttons " were meant for a like use, but on careful examination we could find no trace of pitch or other adhesive matter clinging to any of them; furthermore their bottoms are always excellently finished and show, indeed, more polish than do the sides, whereas objects primarily designed to be glued or cemented to other objects, are generally roughened on those parts which were destined to receive the adhesive substance. This, and the fact that we have three separate sets of exactly seven each, has inclined us to believe that they were some form of dice and that their employment as an embellishment for the tips of the peculiar paired bones may have been a secondary one.

MEDICINE POUCHES OF SKIN

Under this heading are included a number of skin bags of various shapes and sizes which were found with burials. They contained assortments of miscellaneous material, much of it of no apparent practical value.[1] As to whether or not the identification of these sacks as medicine pouches is correct, the reader may judge for himself.

Bag and Contents. The container figured on plate 38, a, is made from prairie-dog skins with the hair on, cut and fitted to form a triangular sack 11 inches long, 10 inches across the base, and $3\frac{1}{2}$ inches across the mouth. The skins are arranged so that the heads

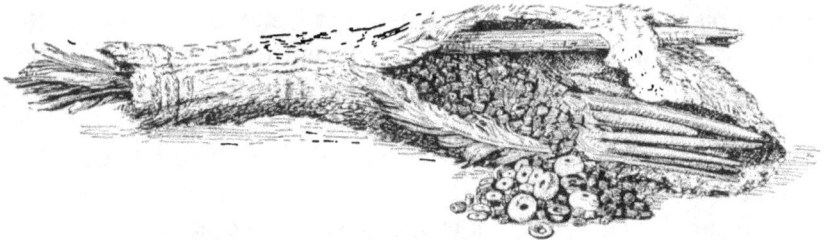

FIGURE 16
Skin bag containing beads and feathers, White Dog Cave. ($\frac{1}{2}$.)

form the mouth of the bag. They are sewn together with a running stitch, the seam inside, the hair side out. Within were a cake of paint, b, and a very small skin bag, c, wrapped with string and holding powdered paint of a brilliant green color. The cake was made of the same paint, apparently moistened and molded into its present shape with the fingers.

Bag with Colored Minerals. This is a little skin container in which were found about twenty small unworked fragments of azurite and malachite.

Dice Bags. These were both taken from Cist 24, White Dog Cave. They are little buckskin bags; each contained seven of the peculiar compound " dice " described above.

Sack with Beads and Feathers. This specimen is illustrated in figure 16. It is a bag of what appears to be badger skin with the hair on, which is somewhat rotted and has split down the side. In

[1] Similar assortments were found with Sayodneechee burials. Kidder-Guernsey, 1919, p. 30.

it are about a teacup full of small cylindrical black seed beads; a few discoidal bone beads; and six large flat stone beads, two of which are of alabaster. There are also eleven large hawk feathers and a section 7 inches long broken from the stalk of a plant with a pithy stem.

Pouch and Small Articles. This heterogeneous assemblage (plate 44) was found in the woven bag shown in plate 30, d, taken from Cave 6. Some of the objects were loose in the woven bag, the remainder were contained in the little skin pouch, a, of the former plate. The latter is made from a piece of thin animal hide, soft dressed with the hair on, folded to form a small, narrow sack 5 inches long, and sewn with fiber string. After having been sewn it was turned to bring the seam inside. A buckskin tie-string is attached to the top. Only traces of the fur remain.

The objects found loose in the woven bag are: a fragment of a fossilized mammalian tooth, b; a piece of hard yellow ochre showing rubbing facets, and grooves such as might have been made by coloring a cord, and in spots, a curious gloss, c; a small lump of organic substance resembling dried fruit, d; and half of a squash seed, f.

In the little skin pouch were: a part of the horny claw cover of an animal, presumably dog or wolf, i; an oval bone die, g, similar to those figured in our first report,[1] except that both sides are convex, instead of one being convex and one flat; a wooden die of bi-convex shape with one surface coated with pitch as in the 1915 examples just referred to, h. The remaining specimen from the pouch is a section 2¾ inches long cut from a grease-wood stick, e. The ends are rounded and wrapped with sinew, and a groove runs the whole length of the under side, the entire object having been painted a dull red.

SUMMARY AND CONCLUSIONS

Summary of Material Culture. Of the dwellings of the Basket-makers we know next to nothing. Certain crudely-built stone structures in Goat Cave (plate 2, a, b) may be Basket-maker, but the evidence is not conclusive. In Cave 14 were found cists made of large slabs and closed over with conical wood and adobe roofs;

---

[1] Kidder-Guernsey, 1919, p. 189 and plate 86, g.

these were built above ground and against the cliff-wall (plate 9, e, f). There is little doubt in our minds that they are Basket-maker products, and they have a distinctly house-like appearance; but their very small size argues for their use as storage places rather than as domiciles. We believe at present, therefore, that the Basket-makers lived mostly in perishable structures built in the open, and only resorted to the caves for temporary shelter in severe weather.

Although they apparently did not live regularly in the caves, they took full advantage of them for the storage of their crops and for the burial of their dead. For both purposes they used cists. These occur in several well-defined varieties (see plate 9). Where the cave floor was of solid hard-pan they excavated plain, jar-shaped cavities in it; some of these have little tunnels or " flues " leading to smaller, shallower holes set about their mouths. When the floor of the cave was of material so loose as to render the above forms unpractical, they scooped out holes, larger or smaller according to their requirements, and lined them with large, flat, stone slabs to hold back the sand. These are the commonest types, and served, apparently, either for storage or burial. Semi-subterranean (Cave 2, 1915), or above-ground cists (Cave 14) with slab foundations and adobe superstructures complete the list; we have so far not found burials in them.

Burial customs were very uniform; the bodies were flexed, wrapped in fur-string blankets and twined-woven bags, and deposited, with numerous mortuary offerings, in the cists. Interments were almost never single; in most cases two to four individuals were buried together.

The Basket-makers grew corn of a single, apparently primitive, variety; squashes also were raised, but the most careful search has so far failed to reveal any evidence of bean culture. The turkey was probably not domesticated. The people covered themselves with robes of fur cloth and dressed hides; men wore a breech-cloth and "gee-string"; the women a short string skirt. The usual footgear was the square-toed sandal, a type which differs from all others in the Southwest in shape, in the presence of a toe-fringe, and in the fact that the soles of the better specimens are provided with a looped " pile " reinforcement covering their entire length.

Children and the adults of both sexes were well supplied with necklaces of stone and shell beads, as well as with pendants of stone and abalone shell; turquoise, apparently, was unknown. Hair-dressing in the case of males was elaborate. The back hair was gathered into a short chubby knot to which was fastened a thin braided scalp-lock falling from the crown of the head; there was often a wide " part" and a tonsure from which the hair was clipped close. Women seem to have worn the hair short; their heads may have provided the great quantity of human hair that was used for string.

Cradles were of two types: the rigid, with wooden frame, twig or reed backing, and padded edge; and the flexible, made of grass or cedar bark. Young babies were always provided with stuffed pads, bound to the navel to prevent rupture.

Basketry was very abundant indeed, but was exclusively of the coiled variety, with two-rod-and-bundle foundation, and with wooden sewing splints. The weave is coarse, but even and very firm; decoration is in black or black-and-red; the designs have a sort of family resemblance to those of the modern tribes of central and northern California. The principal forms are trays, bowls and large panniers. No wickerwork, twined or checker-work baskets were found.

Of textile fabrics, these people turned out very limited amounts of apocynum string cloth, plain over-and-under weave. It was undoubtedly woven on some form of loom, but the small size of the individual pieces produced and the crude nature of the selvages give the impression that the art of loom weaving was still in its infancy. This theory is strengthened by the fact that the designs were either painted on the fabric or made by rubbing color onto the wefts as they were being woven, rather than produced, as in more perfected systems, by the use of separate wefts dyed before insertion. The most elaborate textiles are the hand-twined bags, usually made of apocynum string, and decorated by painting or by rubbing color on the wefts in process. The abundance of such bags is very striking. Although an enormous quantity of finely spun string was employed for the textiles and for a variety of other purposes (such as in rabbit-nets, string aprons, fur cloth, etc.), we have never found any trace of the use of a spindle, either plain or whorled. Fur cloth was much used, true feather-cloth never.

Skin was well dressed and entered into many industries, but most strikingly so in the making of all sorts of small to medium sized bags and pouches, the most characteristic of which are sacks formed of two to seven or eight prairie-dog hides sewed together in such a way that the heads of the animals arranged side by side formed the necks of the bags.

The Basket-makers had few superiors in the careful working of wood; their weapons and implements show as fine shapes and as perfect finish as can be achieved with stone tools. The most typical objects are the atlatl and dart (used, apparently, to the entire exclusion of the bow and arrow); the grooved club; and the crooked shafted, plain-gripped digging stick.

Artifacts of stone are very poorly represented in the collection. There are no specimens of the following types, all common in the cliff-houses and pueblos: axes, both grooved and grooveless, hammer stones, polishing stones, " sandal lasts," chipped scrapers, arrowheads, or long drills. As these lacking forms are all strictly utilitarian in function, their absence may be due to our material being almost exclusively from graves and temporary cave-shelters, rather than from long inhabited dwelling places. It would not surprise us, however, to find that the grooved axe was unknown to the Basket-makers, as that implement among the northern Cliff-dwellers is always of a rude, unspecialized type and therefore presumably of late introduction. The grooved axe is, indeed, entirely absent from the areas to the west and northwest of the Pueblo district.

Of such stone objects as do occur, the most characteristic are the heavy discoidal and sub-spherical beads, the short squat pipes and the large, triangular, tanged dart-points. The chipping of the latter, and of certain large flint knife-blades, is very skillfully done.

Bone tools, like those of stone, are not common in our collection; there are a few simple awls, a few beads, some whistles, and some pairs of decorated tubes which we have classed as ceremonial. There are no bone scrapers. The rarity of awls, among the remains of a people who produced as much coiled basketry as did the Basket-makers, is very peculiar; it is probably due to the fact that we have not yet succeeded in finding long-occupied dwelling places.

While feathers played an unimportant part in the making of robes, having been used only for fringes and ornamental borders, they were much employed in the making of all sorts of ceremonial paraphernalia, as well as for the winging of atlatl darts. Bundles of large feathers, destined probably for the latter purpose, were found in several caves.

True pottery, as far as we know, was not made. The only specimens of burned clay that we have are two small pipes found in 1914–1915. In the present report is described a fragment of an unfired dish with basket marked exterior; this may represent a very primitive form of pottery. In which case again we feel the lack of material from village sites, as it is possible that pottery really did exist but that it never, for some reason, found its way into the graves.

As to pictographs, we only know that the painting of large square-shouldered human figures on the walls of caves was a typical, and apparently an exclusive Basket-maker practice. We have never been able to identify any pecked pictographs as of Basket-maker origin.

Conclusions. Before entering into any discussion of the place of the Basket-makers in the general scheme of Southwestern archaeology, it must first be demonstrated that their culture is really a distinct one. If this cannot be done, if the so-called Basket-maker remains from Grand Gulch and the Kayenta region are to be considered as only a specialized local phase of the widespread Pueblo-Cliff-dweller civilization, then they naturally cease to have any chronological or morphological interest. The authors, however, feel sure that such is not the case; a summary of the evidence follows.

The cliff-houses and pueblos of this region are stone-built dwellings of coursed masonry, laid up with adobe mortar; the rooms are rectangular. Corn of several varieties was cultivated, as well as beans and cotton; the turkey was domesticated. Of the minor arts, the most important was pottery making. Equally characteristic are: twilled yucca leaf sandals, twilled rush matting, and twilled ring-baskets, cotton loom cloth, turkey-feather string, and the bow and arrow. These objects, together with pottery, make up nine-tenths of any collection from the cliff-houses. Turning to the graves, we find that Cliff-dweller skulls were always artificially flattened at the back, and that the bodies, accompanied by generous offerings of pottery, were interred in individual graves, usually in the open.

The Basket-makers, on the other hand, certainly built no houses of coursed masonry; they may, in fact, have possessed no more permanent dwellings than do the Navajo of today. Their corn was of a single, rather primitive, variety; they were ignorant, apparently, of beans and cotton, nor did they domesticate the turkey. They made no pottery worthy of the name (or if they did, it never found its way into the graves), and all the other characteristic Cliff-dweller specimens mentioned above are conspicuous by their absence. They are replaced, however, by such equally characteristic Basket-maker products as the square-toed sandal, the twined-woven bag, and the atlatl. The heads of the Basket-makers were never artificially deformed. The graves, instead of being in the open, were cists excavated in the hard-pan or the sandy fill of caves, and from two or three to ten or more bodies were placed in each cist. Mortuary offerings were numerous and varied, but the one invariable gift to the dead was coiled basketry.

In the above summaries only the leading traits of the two cultures are catalogued. A more detailed comparison in tabular form has been published elsewhere,[1] but enough is here presented to show the essential differences between them, particularly when it is considered that all finds of each class have always run true to form: pottery, for example, and deformed skulls have never appeared in Basket-maker graves; the rubbish of cliff-houses has never given evidence of the manufacture of, for instance, twined-woven bags or the atlatl.

We may now take up the question of age. Here again we are on firm ground. The Basket-makers definitely antedated the Pueblo-Cliff-dweller people. This was stated long ago by the Wetherills and McLloyd and Graham,[2] and was proved to us by the superposition of Cliff-dweller remains upon Basket-maker burials in Sunflower Cave. Even without this clear stratigraphic evidence, the case was reasonably certain, for in several of the other sites investigated we found cliff-house pots or sherds in surface-sand overlying Basket-maker burials but never in the graves themselves. Furthermore, during the 1915 work in Sunflower Cave there was

---

[1] Kidder-Guernsey, 1919, p. 204.   [2] Pepper, 1902.

taken from the cliff-house rubbish a square-toed Basket-maker sandal.[1]

We have proved, to our own satisfaction at least, that the Basket-makers were a people culturally distinct from the Cliff-dwellers; and also that they antedated the latter. At this point definite knowledge ceases; and to the very important questions of the origin of the Basket-maker culture, and of its relation to that of the Cliff-dwellers, we can supply only conjectural answers.

As to origin, it may be said that several traits, such as corn growing and the use of the atlatl, point toward Mexico. The peculiar curved, grooved hand-club, and the method of hair-dressing were both features of the somewhat Mexicanized Maya culture of late prehistoric and early historic times in Yucatan. Furthermore, the only archaeological finds which remind one of the Basket-makers have come from the Coahuila caves in northern Mexico, and from the Tularosa caves in southern New Mexico. The latter sites lie roughly half way between the Kayenta region and Coahuila. Just how much weight should be attached to these bits of evidence we do not know, but it seems to us certain that germs of the culture worked northward from the Mexican highlands in very early times.

Although the question of their origin is obscure, we know at least that the Basket-makers were living in the lower San Juan country prior to the opening of the Pueblo-Cliff-dweller period. As to the relations of the cultures two hypotheses suggest themselves: first, that the Basket-makers were a distinct people who were crowded out of the region by the arrival of their more highly developed successors; second, that they were the direct ancestors of the latter.

If the first hypothesis be correct we need not postulate any great time interval between the two cultures; as one came in, the other was destroyed or moved away. If, on the other hand, we believe that the one developed from the other, we must be prepared to allow a very considerable time for the transition, for there are many radical differences between the cultures; and we have so far

---

[1] This illustrates an important principle of archaeological evidence, viz.: Given two cultures, A and B, in the same area; if A objects are found in B sites, but B objects never in A sites, A may be safely considered older than B. The sporadic finding of Basket-maker products in cliff-houses may be expected in the future, particularly as it is probable that the frequent spoliation of Basket-maker burials was the work of the Cliff-dwellers.

sought in vain for any trait running from the one to the other through an unbroken logical and surely demonstrable evolution. While there are missing links in every such chain, it is possible that in this case some of them may yet be supplied by the hitherto little-known "pre-pueblo" or "slab-house" sites that archaeologists are beginning to uncover in various parts of the Southwest. All such sites hitherto examined have, however, been found in the open and so have yielded no specimens of a perishable nature; hence they have provided us with no evidence as to basketry, sandals, food products or wood-working, the very phases of material culture with which we are most familiar in the case of the Basket-makers and which we therefore most need for comparative and developmental studies. A rigorous search should accordingly be made for " pre-pueblo " habitations and graves in locations where they may be expected to be found protected from moisture. If such are discovered, it should be an easy matter, in view of our accurate knowledge of both the Basket-makers and the developed Cliff-dwellers, to determine definitely whether or not the " pre-pueblo " people were culturally intermediate between them.

To return to the first hypothesis, namely, that the Basket-makers were crowded out of the region by the Cliff-dwellers, and settled somewhere along its edges. We have examined collections from many modern southwestern tribes who possess cultures of about the same grade as that of the Basket-makers, in the hope that we might find some evidence of their descent from the ancient people. Nothing definite could, however, be established, although similarities in basketry, rabbit-nets, and hair ornaments were noticed in the Paiute collections; and, among the Mohave material, in the form and weave of twined bags and in the practice of plugging with wood the quills of feathers. Too much significance, however, must not be placed upon similarities such as the above, for the remarkable state of preservation of the Basket-maker material makes it appear so much like a collection from an existing tribe that it is particularly easy to fall into the way of drawing technological comparisons between it and modern articles, losing sight of the fact that the Basket-maker products are really of great antiquity and that the Paiute, Mohave, and other collections are things of yesterday. Where similarities occur, therefore, their significance as showing direct connection is open to question; the long time interval has permitted the working of too many as yet unassayable factors of culture-growth and transmission.

It may seem to the reader that we have been unduly cautious in our failure to draw any definite conclusions. The work, however, is just beginning, and it is our desire to do no more than record for other students the evidence so far accumulated, and to present the few speculations as to its meaning which we have allowed ourselves to indulge in.

BIBLIOGRAPHY

ALLEN, GLOVER M.
1920. *Dogs of the American Aborigines.* Bulletin of the Museum of Comparative Zoölogy at Harvard College, vol. lxiii, no. 9. Cambridge, 1920.

CATLIN, GEORGE.
1842. *Letters and Notes on the Manners, Customs and Condition of the North American Indians.* New York, 1842.

CUMMINGS, BYRON.
1910. *The Ancient Inhabitants of the San Juan Valley.* Bulletin of the University of Utah, 2nd Archaeological number, vol. 3, pt. 2. Salt Lake City, 1910.

CUSHING, FRANK HAMILTON.
1886. *A Study of Pueblo Pottery as Illustrative of Zuñi Culture Growth.* Fourth Report of the Bureau of Ethnology, pp. 467–521. Washington, 1886.
1895. *The Arrow.* American Anthropologist, vol. viii, no. 4, pp. 307–349. Washington, 1895.

GREGORY, HERBERT E.
1916. *The Navajo Country.* United States Geological Survey, Water-supply Paper, no. 380. Washington, 1916.

HEYE, GEORGE H.
1919. *Certain Aboriginal Pottery from Southern California.* Indian Notes and Monographs; Museum of the American Indian, Heye Foundation, vol. vii, no. 1. New York, 1919.

HOFFMAN, WALTER JAMES.
1896. *The Menomini Indians.* Fourteenth Report of the Bureau of American Ethnology, pp. 1–328. Washington, 1896.

HOLMES, W. H.
1919. *Handbook of Aboriginal American Antiquities. Part I, Introductory. The Lithic Industries.* Bulletin 60, Bureau of American Ethnology. Washington, 1919.

HOOTON, E. A. and WILLOUGHBY, C. C.
1920. *Indian Village Site and Cemetery near Madisonville, Ohio.* Papers of the Peabody Museum of American Archaeology and Ethnology, Harvard University, vol. viii, no. 1. Cambridge, 1920.

BIBLIOGRAPHY

HOUGH, WALTER.
  1914. *Culture of the Ancient Pueblos of the Upper Gila River Region, New Mexico and Arizona.* Bulletin 87, U. S. National Museum. Washington, 1914.
  1919. *The Hopi Indian Collections in the United States National Museum.* Proceedings of the U. S. National Museum, vol. 54, pp. 235–296. Washington, 1919.

KIDDER, A. V. and GUERNSEY, S. J.
  1919. *Archaeological Explorations in Northeastern Arizona.* Bulletin 65, Bureau of American Ethnology. Washington, 1919.

KROEBER, A. L.
  1908. *Ethnology of the Gros Ventre.* Anthropological Papers of the American Museum of Natural History, vol. i, pt. 4. New York, 1908.

LUMHOLTZ, CARL.
  1903. *Unknown Mexico.* London, 1903.

MASON, OTIS TUFTON.
  1904. *Aboriginal American Basketry, Studies in a Textile Art without Machinery.* Annual Report of the U. S. National Museum for 1902, pp. 171–548. Washington, 1904.

MORRIS, EARL H.
  1919. *The Aztec Ruin.* Anthropological Papers of the American Museum of Natural History, vol. xxvi, pt. 1. New York, 1919.

  1919, a. *Preliminary Account of the Antiquities of the Region between the Mancos and La Plata Rivers in Southwestern Colorado.* Thirty-third Report of the Bureau of American Ethnology, pp. 155–206. Washington, 1919.

NORDENSKIÖLD, GUSTAV.
  1893. *The Cliff-Dwellers of the Mesa Verde.* Translated by D. Lloyd Morgan. Stockholm, 1893.

PARSONS, ELSIE CLEWS.
  1918. *War God Shrines of Laguna and Zuñi.* American Anthropologist, n. s. vol. 20, no. 4, pp. 381–405. Lancaster, Pa., 1918.

PEPPER, GEORGE H.
  1902. *The Ancient Basket Makers of Southeastern Utah.* American Museum Journal, vol. ii, no. 4, suppl. New York, 1902.
  1905. *The Throwing Stick of a Prehistoric People of the Southwest.* International Congress of Americanists, 13th Session, New York, 1902, pp. 107–130. Easton, Pa., 1905.

POPE, SAXTON T.
  1918. *Yahi Archery.* University of California Publications in American Archaeology and Ethnology, vol. 13, no. 3. Berkeley, 1918.

BIBLIOGRAPHY

POWELL, J. W.
1875. *Exploration of the Colorado River of the West and its Tributaries. Explored in 1869, 1870, 1871, and 1872.* Washington, 1875.

PRUDDEN, T. MITCHELL.
1897. *An Elder Brother to the Cliff-Dweller.* Harper's Monthly Magazine for June, 1897, pp. 56–63. New York, 1897.
1903. *The Prehistoric Ruins of the San Juan Watershed in Utah, Arizona, Colorado, and New Mexico.* American Anthropologist, n.s., vol. 5, no. 2, pp. 224–288. Lancaster, Pa., 1903.
1907. *On the Great American Plateau.* New York, 1907.

RAU, CHARLES.
1876. *The Archaeological Collection of the U. S. National Museum.* Smithsonian Contributions to Knowledge, no. 287. vol. xxii, Washington, 1876.

SAUNDERS, CHARLES FRANCIS.
1912. *The Indians of the Terraced Houses.* New York, 1912.

SCHELLHAS, PAUL.
1904. *Comparative Studies in the Field of Maya Antiquities.* Bulletin 28, Bureau of American Ethnology. Washington, 1904.

WATERMAN, T. T.
1918. *The Yana Indians.* University of California Publications in American Archaeology and Ethnology, vol. xiii, no. 2. Berkeley, 1918.

www.ingramcontent.com/pod-product-compliance
Lightning Source LLC
Chambersburg PA
CBHW070805280326
41934CB00012B/3071